CADOGAN
island guides

W9-BRY-064

THE IONIAN ISLANDS

Cadogan Books plc
London House, Parkgate Road, London SW11 4NQ

The Globe Pequot Press
6 Business Park Road, PO Box 833, Old Saybrook, Connecticut 06475–0833

Copyright © Dana Facaros 1994
Contributors: Guy Dimond, Stephanie Ferguson and Sarah Hey

Illustrations © Pauline Pears 1986, Suzan Kentli 1993 and Horatio Monteverde 1994

Design by Animage
Cover illustration by Toby Morrison
Maps © Cadogan Guides, drawn by Thames Cartographic Ltd
Macintosh: Jacqueline Lewin and Typography 5

Editing: Guy Dimond
Managing: Vicki Ingle
Editorial Assistant: Emma Johnson
Proofreading: Stewart Wild

Series Editors: Rachel Fielding and Vicki Ingle

ISBN 0–947754–85–7

A catalogue record for this book is available from the British Library
Library of Congress Cataloging-in-Publication-Data available

Printed and bound by Scotprint Ltd,
Musselburgh, Scotland.

About the Author

Dana Facaros is a professional travel writer. Over the past ten years she has lived in several countries, concentrating on the Mediterranean area. In collaboration with her husband Michael Pauls she has written more than a dozen Cadogan Guides on, amongst others, Italy, Spain, France and Turkey. Her roots, however, are in the Greek Islands; her father comes from Ikaria. Dana's guide to all the Greek Islands, now in its fifth edition, was first published in 1979.

About the Contributors

Guy Dimond is a freelance travel writer and editor. He has visited most of the islands featured in this guide, and is editor of the series of Cadogan Guides to the Greek Islands. Freelance journalist and travel writer **Stephanie Ferguson** has travelled extensively throughout Greece and hopped round more than 40 islands. She fell under the spell of the country after a holiday in the Peloponnese in 1976, and since then has contributed to two guide books and has written features on Greece for a number of UK national publications. **Sarah Hey,** former editor of the English-language newspaper the *Corfu News*, has delivered yachts between the Ionian Islands and Mainland Greece. She is currently feature-writer on the *Yorkshire Evening Post*.

Author's Acknowledgements

I would like to thank the many members of the National Tourist Organization of Greece for their kind assistance in writing this guide, and the following people without whose moral, physical and financial assistance it would not have been possible: my parents and my grandmother, Mrs Despina Facaros, Joseph Coniaris, Sotiros S. Kouvaras of Ithaki, Filia and Kosta Pattakos, Carolyn Steiner and Julie Wegner. A special thanks goes to my better half, Michael, who added the bull; to my aunt and Ikariote informant Toula Cavaligos; and to Guy, Stephanie and Sarah for their invaluable amendments and additions.

Contents

Travel · 1–22

Practical A–Z · 23–46

Modern History, Art and Architecture   47–58

Topics   59–69

Athens and Piraeus   71–95

Maps

What weighs the bosom of Abraham and the immaterial spectres of Christian paradise against this Greek eternity made of water, rock and cooling winds?

Kazantzakis

Introduction

There's nothing like the Greek islands to make the rest of the world seem blurred, hesitant and grey. Their frontiers are clearly defined by a sea that varies from emerald and turquoise to indigo blue, with none of the sloppiness of a changing tide; the clear sky and dry air cut their mountainous contours into sharp outline; the whiteness and simplicity of their architecture is both abstract and organic. Even the smells, be they fragrant (lemon blossoms, incense, wild thyme, grilling fish) or whiffy (donkey flops, caique diesel engines, plastic melted cheese sandwiches) are pure and unforgettable. In such an environment, the islanders themselves have developed strong, open characters; they have bright eyes and are quick to laugh or cry or scream in fury, or enquire into the most intimate details of your personal life and offer unsolicited lectures on politics, how to brush your teeth properly or find a good husband.

Since the 1970s this clarity has been a magnet to tourists from the blurred, hesitant, grey world beyond. After shipping, tourism is Greece's most important source of income, to the extent that swallows from the north have become a regular fixture in the seasonal calendar: first comes Lent and Greek Easter, then the tourists, followed by the grape harvest, and in December, the olives. From June to September, ferries and flights are packed with holidaymakers, both Greek and foreign. Popular sites and beaches are crowded by day, and often by night as well, by visitors unable to find a room—they've been booked for months in advance.

Yet as each island has its own character, each has responded to the tourism cash cow in a slightly different way. On some, resort hotels have toadstooled up willy-nilly in search of the fast package-tour buck; some islands have sacrificed many charming old customs, environmental health, and even sanity itself in their desire to please all comers. And then there are other islands and villages, more self-reliant, clinging stubbornly to their traditions and doing all they can to keep outside interests from exploiting their coasts. Others, including some of the most visited islands, are enjoying a renaissance of traditional arts and customs, often led by the young who are pained to see their centuries-old heritage eroding into Euro-blandness.

If this book has any real purpose, it's to help you find the island of your dreams, whether you want all the mod-cons of home, sports facilities and disco dancing until dawn, or want to visit the ancient sites, study Byzantine frescoes and hone up on your Greek, or perhaps just escape to a secluded shore, where there's the luxury of doing nothing at all. Or perhaps you want a bit of each. For, in spite of all the rush to join the 20th century, the Greek islands have retained the enchantment that inspired Homer and Byron—the wine-dark sea, the scent of jasmine at twilight and nights alive with shooting stars.

The ancient Greeks dedicated the islands to the gods, and they have yet to surrender them entirely to us mortals. They have kept something pure and true and alive. Or as the poet Palamas wrote, 'Here reigns nakedness. Here shadow is a dream'.

The Ionian Islands

The seven islands scattered randomly across the Ionian sea, from Corfu in the north to Kythera at the southern end of the Peloponnese, have been lumped together politically since Byzantine times. Off the western frontier of Greece, they share a unique history, and generally speaking, are more Italianate, more lush, and in temperament less prone to the extremes that bewitch and bedazzle the rest of the country. They also get more rain, especially from October to March, only to be rewarded with a breathtaking bouquet of wild flowers in the spring and autumn, especially on Corfu.

Weather and history aside, the Ionian islands each have such a strong, distinct personality that any further generalities may safely be sent packing. Because connections between the islands, once almost non-existent, are more frequent in the summer, you can easily hop from one to the next depending on your mood, whether you want to boogie the night away in a Zakynthos nightclub, windsurf below the cliffs at Lefkas, or seek Odysseus' beloved home on Ithaca.

Choosing Your Island

The 3000 islands of Greece (of which a mere 170 or so are inhabited) are divided into seven major groupings: the Cyclades in the Aegean, surrounding the holy island of Delos; the Dodecanese, lying off the southwest coast of Asia Minor; the Northeastern Aegean islands, stretching from Thassos to Ikaria; the Saronic islands, in the Saronic Gulf; the Sporades, spread off the coast of Thessaly and Evia; Crete, the largest island in Greece; and the Ionian islands, sprinkled between Greece and Italy.

An overall picture of the Ionian islands may help you pinpoint likely destinations. You may want to head for a lively cosmopolitan place, followed by a few days of absolute peace and quiet. Below are thumbnail sketches, starting with the liveliest, trendiest and most touristy.

The great queen of Greek tourism, **Corfu**, is large enough to absorb huge numbers of tourists, but suffers from pockets of mass package tourism of the least attractive type. Stay clear of those spots and there's plenty left. It has a stunning capital and charming mountain villages. The lovely island of **Zakynthos** has lost much of its original character under the strain of mass package tourism, but there's plenty going on to keep you amused. Arguably the best type of island holiday can be found on islands where there are enough tourists to ensure more than basic facilities—places with a choice of decent tavernas, a bar or two for an evening drink, and most of all, a place to sit out and watch life idle by. **Kefalonia** and **Lefkas** fall happily into this category; both have a mixture of rugged island scenery, typical villages, good restaurants and swimming. There are special gems like little **Paxos**, with its sheltered bays, harbours and coves, a haven for sailors. There remain a few Greek islands that come under the heading of 'almost away from it all'—not quite your desert island in that they have several places to stay, eat and explore, but beyond that not a lot to do after a couple of days, unless you are resourceful—**Kythera** is a good example of this.

If, however, you genuinely want to get away from it all and don't mind eating in the same little taverna every night, then head for **Ithaca**. You can treat yourself to some serious introspection and brush up on your modern Greek with the locals.

When to Go

Individually the seven Ionian islands are quite distinct, both geologically and in character. Even connections between the Ionians were long scanty at best. Now—at least in the summer—you can with relative ease visit six of them, and there's a ferry to Italy (usually to Brindisi, Ancona or Bari) from Corfu, Paxos, Kefalonia and Ithaca.

In the off season getting around becomes more difficult. Not only do ships sail less frequently, but from late October to March heavy rains are the rule. They give the Ionian islands a lushness the Aegean islands lack; springtime, especially in Corfu, is breathtaking, and the autumn wild flowers are nearly as beautiful as those in spring. Summers, however, tend to be hot, lacking the natural air conditioning provided by the meltemi on Greece's eastern shores.

When choosing your island(s), the time of the year is of paramount importance, and from mid-July to 20 August you can expect nothing but frustration on the more popular islands, or the smaller ones with a limited number of beds. Don't assume that the more isolated the island or resort the cheaper the accommodation, as supply and demand dictate the prices. Out of season you can pick and choose, and places with a high percentage of Greek tourists, who tend to go for a 6-week burst in the height of summer, are a bargain.

History

Lying between Greece and Italy, the Ionian islands have spent centuries out of the mainstream of Greek politics, although from the beginning their inhabitants have been Hellene to the core. Not to be confused with Ionia in Asia Minor (named for the Ionians' legendary father Ios, son of Apollo), the Ionian sea and islands are named after Io the priestess, who caught the roving eye of Zeus. When the jealous Hera was about to catch the couple in flagrante delicto Zeus changed the girl into a white cow, but Hera was not fooled. She asked Zeus to give her the cow as a present, and ordered the sleepless hundred-eyed Argus to watch over her. With the help of Hermes, who charmed Argus to sleep and killed him, Io escaped, only to be pursued by a terrible stinging gad-fly sent by Hera. The first place through which she fled has ever since been named the Ionian Sea in honour of the tormented girl.

Very little remains of the ancient past on the islands, although they were probably settled in the Stone Age by people from Illyria (present-day Albania) and then by the Eretrians. Homer was the first to mention them, and were he the last they would still be immortal as the homeland of crafty Odysseus. In the 8th century BC, mercantile Corinth colonized the islands. As trade expanded between Greece and the Greek colonies in southern Italy and Sicily, the islands became ever more important; Corfu, the richest, grew so high and mighty that she defeated mother Corinth at sea, and proclaimed herself the ally of Athens. This forced Sparta, Corinth's ally, either to submit to this expansion of the Athenian Empire and control of western trade through the Ionians islands, or to attack. They attacked. The result was the disastrous Peloponnesian War.

The Romans incorporated the Ionian islands into their province Achaia (still the current name of the province). After the fall of the Roman Empire, the Ostrogoths from Italy overran the islands, only to be succeeded by the Byzantines, who fortified them for their strategic importance as a bridge between Constantinople and Rome. In 1084, during the Second Crusade, however, the Normans under Duke Robert Guiscard of Sicily took the islands by surprise and established bases to plunder the rest of Greece. With a great deal of difficulty the Byzantines succeeded in forcing them out of Corfu at least, although the Normans were no sooner gone when the Venetians claimed the islands in the land grab after the Sack of Constantinople in 1204. The southern islands became the County Palatine of Kefalonia when Venice put an end to the claims of the Sicilian Norman pirate, Vetrano, by crucifying him. Fate, however, dealt Corfu into the hands of the grasping Angevins for 150 years, a rule so bitter that the inhabitants surrendered their island to the 'protection' of Venice.

Venetian rule was hardly a bed of roses. The average Greek in fact preferred the Turks to the bossy Catholic 'heretics': if nothing else, the Turks allowed the people a measure of self-government and demanded fewer taxes. Some of the Ionian islands came under Turkish rule until 1499, and the Ottomans renewed the assaults as Serenissima weakened. For all their faults, the Venetians were at least more tolerant of artists than the Turks, and in the 17th century the Ionian islands became a refuge for painters, especially from Crete. The resulting Ionian school was noted for its fusion of Byzantine and Renaissance styles.

In 1796, Napoleon conquered Venice; as the Ionian islands were of the utmost importance to his schemes of conquest he demanded them with the Treaty of Campo Formio. In 1799 a combined Russo-Turkish fleet took the islands from him, creating the independent Septinsular Republic under their protection—not only from the French but from the notorious tyrant of Epirus, Ali Pasha, who coveted them. Although the Septinsular Republic was nullified by the 1807 Treaty of Tilsit which returned the islands to Napoleon, it was the first time in almost four centuries that any Greeks anywhere had been allowed a measure of self-rule. Most importantly, it kindled the War of Independence in 1821.

In 1815 the British took the Ionian islands under military protection and reformed the Ionian State, appointing a High Commissioner who took precedence over the Ionian parliament. Sir Thomas Maitland, the first High Commissioner, has gone down in history as one of the most disliked British representatives ever; he assumed dictatorial powers, and deeply offended the Greeks by giving the city of Parga, an important port on the mainland, to the tyrant Ali Pasha, obeying an obscure clause in the 1815 treaty that everyone else had forgotten. Other High Commissioners were little better from the Greek point of view and the Ionian State never stopped demanding or conspiring for union with Greece. Once they had Cyprus, the British agreed to cede the islands to Greece in 1864—but only after blowing up all the fortresses on Corfu. During the Second World War Italy took the islands, but Mussolini's dream of creating a new Ionian State under Italian protection was shattered in 1943 when the Germans occupied the islands. Large numbers of Italian troops joined the Greeks in fighting the Nazis, only to be slaughtered by their former Axis allies. When the news reached Italy, it contributed to the collapse of the fascist government.

Getting To and Around Greece and the Ionian Islands

By Air

If you're travelling from abroad to the Ionian islands, a direct flight is by far the simplest, fastest, and often the cheapest way to get there. Corfu, Kefalonia and Zakynthos (Zante) all have international airports; but if you want to travel via Athens, this is also quite a feasible way of getting there.

Charter Flights

Charter flights have fixed outward and return dates, with the return date in less than one month. They are sold either with a package holiday or through 'consolidators' (travel agents) as a flight only. Charter flights to Athens and to Corfu, Zakynthos or Kefalonia are frequent in the summer from European and North American capitals. Charters direct to Athens are available from Birmingham, Glasgow, Luton, Newcastle and Manchester. In London many travel agents offer cheap last-minute flights, and 'bucket shops' have made spare charter tickets their speciality (a return to Athens for £125 is possible). Look through publications such as *Time Out*, the *Evening Standard* or the Sunday papers for cheap deals. **Americans and Canadians** with more time than money may well find their cheapest way of getting to Greece is to take a trans-Atlantic economy flight to London and from there to buy a last-minute ticket to Greece. This may be difficult in July or August, however. Trans-Atlantic bargains can still be found, but bear in mind that the peak season runs from late May to mid-September.

There are several rules about charters to Greece. One is that a charter ticket is valid for a minimum of two nights and a maximum of four weeks. Visitors to Greece using a charter flight may visit Turkey or any other neighbouring country for the day, but must not stay overnight; the Turkish officials usually stamp your passport showing the dates of entry and exit. Even if you intend to stay longer than four weeks or travel to other countries, using just half a charter ticket may still work out less than a scheduled flight, so shop around.

When you buy a **flight-only charter ticket**, you will be issued with an accommodation voucher, which entitles you to stay at a (sometimes fictitious) hotel. This strange formality is a left-over from the days when charter tickets were only sold with accommodation included. It's unlikely the Greek customs officials will ask to see this voucher, but keep it handy until you're out of the airport just in case. Student or youth charters are exempt from the voucher system and are allowed to be sold as one-way tickets. Travelling this way you can stay for over a month as long as you are under 26 or a full-time, card-carrying student under 32.

Basic travel insurance is sometimes sold with charter tickets to Greece by travel agents. It is not compulsory to buy this, no matter what they might tell you. If they insist, look elsewhere.

Scheduled Flights

Scheduled flights offer greater flexibility than charter flights, but generally cost more. While many charters go direct to the Ionian islands, scheduled flights rarely go there directly from outside Greece; they almost invariably go to Athens, then a connection is needed. Scheduled flights fly direct to Athens daily from London and New York. KLM flies via Amsterdam from Toronto, Montréal, Calgary and Halifax. While the basic carriers from the United States are Olympic Airways TWA, and Delta (via Frankfurt), from London it's Olympic Airways, British Airways or Virgin Atlantic. London offers the greatest variety of flights and the prices are often competitive close to the departure time if you book through a consolidator (travel agent) instead of directly with the airline. It's advisable to shop around and see which offers the best deal. Superpex flights offer substantially reduced fares, with flights from London to Athens ranging from £180 low season to £280 high season. They must, however, be paid for on the spot and are not refundable or flexible. American economy fares range from around $900 New York–Athens in low season to $1300 high season.

Olympic Airways	✆ (071) 409 3400/493 3965 (London)
	✆ (212) 838 3600 (New York)
	✆ (01) 926 7251 (Athens)
British Airways	✆ (081) 897 4000 (London)
Virgin Atlantic	✆ (0293) 747747; info, (0293) 511581 (London)
Delta	✆ (800) 241 4141/(800) 221 1212 (New York)
Aer Lingus	✆ (0232) 245151 (Dublin)
KLM	✆ (514) 933 1314 (Montréal)
TWA	✆ (800) 892 4141 (New York)

Bona-fide students under 26 are sometimes eligible for discounts, especially with Olympic Airways who currently offer 25% discount to ISIC card holders on all connecting flights from Athens to the islands, even when booked from London; **Trailfinders**, 42–50 Earls Court Road, W8 6EJ, ✆ (071) 937 5400,

STA Travel, 86 Old Brompton Road, London SW7 or 117 Euston Road, WC1, ℂ (071) 937 9962; and **Campus Travel**, 52 Grosvenor Gardens, SW1 (071) 730 8111 can get you some of the best current deals. Returning from Greece, it is advisable to confirm your return flight a few days prior to departure.

Flights from Athens to the Ionian Islands

Connecting flights from Athens to the islands are available on Olympic Airways, 11 Conduit Street, London W1R 0LP, ℂ (071) 493 3965. At the time of writing, an additional flat fare of £50 will allow you to connect a flight landing at Athens to Kefalonia, Zakynthos, Corfu, and a handful of other Greek island airports, connections permitting. Preveza airport is nearby on the mainland, with good connections via the port at Aktion; Lefkas is only a half-hour bus journey from the airport. To be assured of a seat, especially in the summer, you should book your ticket as far in advance as possible. Infants up to 2 years old receive a 90% discount, and children of 2–12 years a 50% discount. Students only receive a 25% discount if the flight is a connecting one. Americans who do not have an Olympic Airways office in their town can call a toll-free no. (800) 223 1226 for information.

In recent years Olympic Airways has been offering island-to-island flights in season, a pleasant innovation that precludes the need to go via Athens. Although these have a habit of changing from year to year, routes between Zakynthos and Kefalonia are fairly established. As the newly-privatized Olympic Airways no longer has a monopoly on inter-island flights, it's only a matter of time before other recently-formed Greek airlines set up in competition or try out new routes.

Olympic Airways

6 Othonos; ℂ 929 2555 (Int.), 929 2444 (Dom.).

Also 96 Leoforos Syngrou; ℂ 929 2333.

East Airport ℂ 969 9317.
West Airport ℂ 989 2111.

Getting to and from Ellinikon Airport, Athens

Ellinikon Airport is divided into two: East (international airlines) and West (Olympic Airlines, both international and domestic flights). Double decker blue-and-yellow express buses leave for either terminal (but not both, so be sure you are getting on the right one) from Amalias Avenue, at the top of Syntagma Square, every 20 minutes between 6am and 9pm, every ½-hour between 9pm and 2am, and every hour from 2am to 6am. The fare is 160 dr. from 6am to midnight,

270 dr. otherwise. At the time of writing, this bus stop was being dug up for the new metro station, and the buses temporarily suspended. The alternative, until these buses are reinstated, is the public bus no. 133 from Othonos St, Syntagma Square (5.40am–midnight, every 15 minutes), or no. 122 from Vass. Olgas (5.30am–11.30pm, every 15 minutes); both go to the West terminal only. The fare is 75 dr.

The East terminal may be reached by public bus no. 121 from Vass. Olgas Avenue (6.50am–10.50pm, every 40 minutes; 75 dr.). From Piraeus, express bus no. 19 goes to both the East and West terminals (160 dr.).

The metro is an important means of getting across Athens, especially from Piraeus. It runs to Kifissia stopping at Thissio, Monastiraki, Omonia and Plateia Viktorias. Trolley buses run throughout the city centre from the Larissis station to Omonia and Syntagma and out to Koukaki, or linking Syntagma and Omonia with Patission and the National Archaeological Museum.

Taxis from Athens Airport

A taxi between Athens and the airport should cost you about 1100 dr. (more at night). Piraeus is particularly prone to cowboys preying on unsuspecting tourists heading from and to the ferries. Travellers should make sure they take proper yellow taxis with meters and official licence numbers. The tricksters hassle you (especially at Piraeus, less so at the airport) and charge 2–3,000 dr for the journey; it should be around half that. If there's no meter, watch out. Prices are only double from 1–6am and on holidays such as Easter. You will have to pay surcharges on luggage, 50 dr. a piece, plus a 100 dr. supplement for an airport or Piraeus run.

In Athens cabs are difficult to find during the rush hour, when the drivers are knocking off for lunch, and when everyone is going back to work in the evenings. Hailing a cab is not for the faint-hearted. You almost have to hurl yourself in front of it and yell out your destination. Sharing is common and you all pay the full fare. Just check the meter reading when you get in so you don't get overcharged. Sharing (at full price) is also common on the islands.

By Train

There are no longer any direct trains from London to the Ionian Islands or Athens, partly because of the civil war in former Yugoslavia. It is still possible to get to Corfu or Athens by train, changing en route, if you really want to travel that way; it takes three days. Call **British Rail International** in London, ✆ (071) 834 2345. The route goes through Italy, either to Ancona or further south to Bari or Brindisi, and involves taking the ferry over to Corfu; from there the train continues east to Athens. These are all quite busy routes. British people under the age of 26 can travel by **InterRail** youth passes, which currently cost £249 for a month's rail travel in Europe—which gets you there and back via most places in Europe the train goes (excluding the UK, channel ferries and Spain). InterRail passes are also available to British residents over 26 for either 15 days or a month at around 30% more. Americans and Canadians can buy 2-month **Eurail** and **Youth Eurail** passes before leaving home. However, the Eurail Pass is no bargain if you're only going to Greece, which has a limited rail service. For people over 60, the **Rail Europ** senior card saves up to 30% on rail fares in Greece and several other European countries, in Germany, and on most sea crossings. It costs £5 and can be purchased at any from British Rail by holders of a British Rail card.

The sad truth is that since the war in Yugoslavia, travelling by train is no longer an inexpensive, pleasant or easy method of getting to Greece; it's now cheaper, and a lot more comfortable, to fly. The train does have its uses though if you want to stop off and see some of the rest of Europe en route.

Rail Routes (Domestic)

Athens–Patras (for Ionian Islands)	7 daily
Athens–Kalamata (for Kythera)	5 daily

The railway station for the Peloponnese (the land mass you traverse between Athens and the Ionian islands) is in Delighianni St, ✆ 513 1601, and is not to be confused with the adjacent Larissa station which serves northern Greece. In Piraeus, the station for the Peloponnese is near the Piraeus–Athens metro on Akti Kalimassioti. For further information telephone the OSE (Hellenic Railways Organization): (01) 522 2491 or 362 4402/6. Recorded timetables can be obtained by dialling 145 (for Greece) or 147 (for the rest of Europe).

By Bus

London to Athens

Taking a bus from London to Athens is always a possible alternative for those who are averse to air or train travel. It isn't usually much cheaper than a standby fight. But with 2½ days (or more) on the road and Adriatic ferry, adventures are practically included in the ticket price. **Eurolines**, 52 Grosvenor Gardens, Victoria, London SW1, ✆ (071) 730 0202 offer 3-day journeys from London to Corfu or Athens which cost around £218 return if you're over 26; there's a £12 saving if you're under 26. **Olympic Bus Ltd**, 70 Brunswick Centre, London WC1 1AE, © (071) 837 9141, offer 2½-day journeys from London to Athens via Brussels and Italy for a mere £50 one-way, or £100 return, departing London on Friday evenings. In Greece, you'll find agencies selling bus tickets on the most obscure islands, as well as in Athens; Filellinon St near Syntagma Square is Athens' budget travellers' boulevard, so check there for other possibilities.

Domestic Bus Services

The domestic bus service in Greece is efficient and regular, if not always a bargain. Each bus is decorated at the whim of its drivers, with pin-ups, saints, wallpaper, tinsel, tassels, and plastic hands which wave violently when the bus falls into a pothole. Local buses can be great fun; long-distance journeys are more testing. The journey times to various Greek destinations from Athens are as follows, with departures at least three or four times per day:

Athens to	Terminal	©	Duration
Gythion (Mani, Peloponnese)	Kifissou	512 4913	5.30hrs
Igoumenitsa (for Corfu, Ionian Is.)	Kifissou	512 5954	8.30hrs
Kefalonia (Ionian Islands)	Kifissou	512 9498	8hrs
Kerkyra (Corfu, Ionian Is.)	Kifissou	512 9443	11hrs
Lefkas (Ionian Islands)	Kifissou	513 3583	5.30hrs
Patras (for Ionian Islands)	Kifissou	513 6185	3hrs
Zakynthos	Kifissou	512 9432	7hrs

To get to the terminal at 100 Kifissou St, take bus no. 51 from Omonia Square (Zinonos and Menadrou Sts).

During the summer it is advisable to reserve seats in advance on the long-distance buses. Tickets for these journeys must normally be bought before one boards the bus. Note that Lefkas is joined to the mainland by bridge, which is good to remember if no ferries are running to the islands due to either strikes or bad weather.

There are never enough buses on the islands in the summer nor is it customary to queue. However, you will not be left behind if it is humanly possible for you to squeeze on. If you can wake up in time, you will find that buses are rarely crowded early in the morning.

Within the Athens area the bus fare is 75 dr. You must buy a ticket or book of ten tickets in advance from a kiosk or newsagent, then stamp one to validate it on boarding the bus—if you can fight your way to the machine, that is. If you don't then get caught, you're liable for a fine 20 times the prevailing fare. The trolley buses operate in the same way as normal buses, but on fixed routes.

By Boat

The most common sea route to Greece is from Italy, with daily ferry services from Ancona, Bari, Brindisi, Otranto and Venice, often via the Ionian islands. The most popular of these is the daily service from Brindisi, which leaves at 10pm (connecting with the train from Rome) and arrives in Corfu the next morning. Passengers are allowed a free infinite stopover in Corfu if that island is not their ultimate destination, before continuing to Igoumenitsa or Patras, but make sure it is noted on your ticket. If you plan to sail in the summer, it's advisable to make reservations in advance, especially if you bring a car (most travel agents can do this for you). Students and young people can get a discount of up to 20%. Discounts of up to 20% are also offered when buying a return ticket. The quality of service among the different lines varies, of course; some ships are spanking clean and are plushly furnished—one at least even has a laser disco—while others have been in service so long that they creak. However, the sullen demeanour of the crews seems to be uniform.

An irregular **catamaran** service links Bari with Corfu in under 4 hours, but doesn't take cars.

Ferries

Ports	Frequency	Company
Ancona–Corfu–Patras	2/4 times a week	Strintzis Lines 26 Akti Possidonos Piraeus, ⓒ 412 9815 UK, ⓒ 0883 48511
Ancona–Patras		G.A. Ferries Akti Condili & 2 Aitolikou Piraeus ⓒ 411 0007 UK, ⓒ (071) 836 8216
Ancona–Corfu– Igoumenitsa–Patras	2/4 times a week	ANEK Lines 54 Amalias Avenue Athens, ⓒ 323 3481 UK, ⓒ (081) 452 8231

Ancona–Igoumenitsa–Corfu–Patras	5 times a week	Minoan Lines 2 Vass. Konstantinou Athens, ✆ 751 2356 UK, ✆ 0304 203388
Ancona–Patras	twice a week	Marlines 38 Akti Possidonos Piraeus, ✆ 411 0777 UK, ✆ (081) 452 8231
Brindisi–Corfu–Patras	3 times a week	Hellenic Mediterranean Lines 28 Amalias Avenue Athens, ✆ 323 6333 UK, ✆ (071) 499 0076
Bari–Corfu–Igoumenitsa–Patras	Daily	Ventouris Ferries 26 Amalias Avenue Athens, ✆ 324 0276 UK, ✆ (081) 452 8231
Brindisi–Corfu–Igoumenitsa	Daily	Fragline 5a Rethymnou St Athens, ✆ 822 1285 UK, ✆ (081) 452 8231
Brindisi–Corfu–Igoumenitsa–Patras	Daily	Adriatica 4 Filellinon St Athens, ✆ 322 3693 Italy, ✆ (041) 781611
	Daily	Hellenic Mediterranean Lines (*see* above)
Brindisi–Patras	Daily	Mediterranean Lines 274 Alkiviadou St Piraeus, ✆ 453 1882
Brindisi–Kefalonia–Patras	Daily in summer	Hellenic Mediterranean Lines (*see* above)
Brindisi–Corfu	Daily in summer	Marlines (*see* above)

Boats to the Islands

The daily newspaper *Naftemboriki* lists all the activities of the port at Piraeus and publishes weekly ship schedules. The National Tourist Office also publishes a monthly list of ship departures, both abroad and to the islands.

A little travelling through the islands will soon show you that each boat is an individual. The many new ones are clean and comfortable and often air-conditioned. The older boats may lack some modern refinements but nevertheless they can be pleasant if you remain out on deck. The drinking water is never very good on the boats, but all sell beer, Coca Cola and lemon or orange soda. Biscuits and cigarettes complete the fare on the smaller boats, while the larger ones offer sandwiches, cheese pies or even full meals. Snacks tend to be pricier and of inferior quality to what you'll find on shore. If you're lucky, you'll have *souvlaki* sellers and pedlars offering nuts and *koulouria* (ringed biscuits) as the boat moves from island to island. The smallest boats which ferry you along the coast from beach to beach are called caiques, and usually have no facilities at all.

All the boats are privately owned and although the Greek government controls the prices some will be relatively more expensive, depending on the facilities offered, speed, etc. In most cases children under the age of 4 travel free, and between 4 and 10 for half-fare. Over 10 they are charged the full fare. In the summer it is wise to buy tickets in advance, to guarantee a place, but you can always buy the ticket on board if you haven't had the time. Refunds are rarely given unless the boat itself never arrives, perhaps stuck in Piraeus for tax delinquencies. Boats will arrive late or divert their course for innumerable reasons, so if you have to catch a flight home allow for the eccentricities of the system and leave a day early to be safe.

When purchasing a ticket, either in Piraeus or on the islands, it's always best to do so from your ship's central agency. Other agencies may tell you that the boat is full, when in truth they've merely sold all the tickets allotted them by the central agency. On many islands, agents moonlight as bartenders or grocers and may only have a handwritten sign next to the door advertising their ship's departures.

Most inter-island ferries have three or four classes: the first class, with an air-conditioned lounge and cabins (and often as expensive as flying); the second class, often with its own lounge as well, but smaller cabins; tourist class, with no cabins; and deck class, which is the norm, and usually gives you access to the typically large, stuffy rooms full of 'airline seats' and the snack bar area. As a rule the Greeks go inside and the tourists stay out—on summer nights in particular this is perhaps the most pleasant alternative if you have a sleeping bag.

You'd do well always to keep your ticket with you on a Greek ship, at least until the crew enacts its 'ticket control', a comedy routine necessitated by the fact that Greeks don't always check tickets when passengers board. Instead, after one or two pleas on the ship's loudspeaker system for passengers without tickets to purchase them forthwith, you suddenly find all the doors on the boat locked or guarded by a bored but obdurate sailor, while bands of officers rove about the boat checking tickets. Invariably mix-ups occur: children are separated from their parents, others have gone to the wc, someone has left a ticket with someone on the other side of the immovable sailor, crowds pile up at the doors, and stowaways are marched to the purser's office. In the worst cases, this goes on for an hour; on smaller ships it's usually over in 15 minutes.

Prices, though no longer cheap, are still fairly reasonable for passengers, rather dear for cars.

Hydrofoils

There now appears to be a moderately reliable hydrofoil service service thumping over the seas between the Ionian islands. *Europe I and Europe II* connect Kefalonia, Ithaca, Patras and Zakynthos in various permutations, plus a few small ports (though schedules for these may not settle down for some time yet).

Hydrofoils as a rule travel twice as fast as ships and are twice as expensive (in some cases as much as a plane). In the peak season they are often fully booked, so buy tickets as early as you can. In a choppy sea a trip may leave you saddle-sore, and if the weather is very bad, they don't leave port. All the hydrofoils run throughout the year but are less frequent in winter.

Tourist Excursion Boats

These are generally slick and clean, and have become quite numerous in recent years. They are more expensive than the regular ferries or steamers, but often have schedules that allow visitors to make day excursions to nearby islands (though you can also take them one way), and are convenient, having largely taken the place of the caique operators, many of whom now specialize in excursions to remote beaches instead of island-hopping on request. They may be the only transport available to the most remote islands, but do enquire about scheduled ferries. Friendly yachtsmen may give you a lift—it never hurts to ask.

For the most recent information on Greek sea connections, get a copy of *Greek Travel Pages* by International Publications in Athens, or *Key Travel Guide*, which is updated every week. Travel agents and the Greek National Tourist Offices sometimes have spare copies, and they're easy to find in Greece itself. Better still, the *Thomas Cook Guide to Greek Island Hopping* (£9.99) is excellent for details of ferry services.

By Car

Driving from **London to Athens** (and taking the ferry from Italy to Greece) at a normal pace takes around 3½ days, which is why one sees so few British cars in Greece. Unless you are planning to spend a few weeks covering large distances on land, a car is not really worth the expense and trouble of bringing it to Greece. There are many car hire companies on the mainland and the islands, if you feel a car is necessary; prices are, if anything, higher than the rest of Europe. An **International Driving Permit** is not required by EC citizens carrying an EC driving licence. Other nationals can obtain an International Driving Permit at home, or at one of the Greek Automobile Touring Club offices (ELPA, who charge around £10 for this), by presenting a national driving licence, passport, photograph–and fee of 5000 dr. In practice, tourists with bona-fide US, Australian or European driving licences can usually hire a car without fuss. The minimum age for driving is 18 years; 21 to 25 years for hire. If you're taking your own car, **The Motor Insurance Bureau** at 10 Xenofontos St, Athens, ℃ (01) 323 6733, can tell you which Greek insurance company represents your own, or can provide you with additional cover for Greece.

Customs formalities for bringing in a car are very easy and usually take very little time. A Green Card (international third party insurance) is essential and you will get a carnet stamped in your passport. If your vehicle has EC number plates, you are allowed unlimited free use of your car in Greece. Non-EC vehicles have six months of free use in Greece, and after that you need to apply for a 9-month extension. If you leave Greece without your car, you must have it withdrawn from circulation by a customs authority. ELPA has a list of lawyers who can offer free legal advice on motorcars. They also have a 24-hour recording of information useful to foreign motorists, ✆ 174.

Parking in the centre of Athens is forbidden outside designated parking areas. The traffic situation there is so bad that only cars with even number plates can park one day, cars with odd number plates the next. Local radio and newspapers tell drivers if they're on an odd or even day. Some families cheat by owning two cars. Police can unscrew the licence plates of illegally parked cars, and often do. While driving in the centre of Athens may be a hair-raising experience, most the rest of Greece (busy towns and rough trails excepted) is easy and pleasant. There are few cars on most roads, even in summer, and all signs have their Latin equivalents. Traffic regulations and signalling comply with standard practice on the European Continent (i.e. driving on the right). Flocks of goats or sheep, old ladies on donkeys, and slow-moving lawnmower jitneys are some of the more interesting 'obstructions'. Crossroads and low visibility in the mountains are probably the greatest hazards. Where there are no right of way signs at a cross-roads, give priority to traffic coming from the right, and always beep your horn on blind corners. Take special care when approaching an unguarded railway level crossing. It is also advisable to take a spare container of petrol along with you, as petrol stations are inconsistent in their frequency. There is a speed limit of 50 kph (30 mph) in inhabited areas: other speed limits are indicated by signposts in kilo-metres. Horn blowing is prohibited in Athens and other big cities, though you'd never guess it from the cacophony that starts when the red light changes to green. The Greek Automobile Touring Club (ELPA) operates a breakdown service (free if you've brought your AA/RAC membership card with you) within 60 km (40 miles) of Athens or Patras: dial ✆ 104.

Greek Automobile Touring Club (ELPA)

Athens: 2–4 Messogion St, Tower of Athens, ✆ (01) 779 1615
Corfu: Pat. Athinagora, ✆ (0661) 39504
Patras: Astingos & 127 Korinthou, ✆ (061) 425411 426416

By Motorbike, Moped or Scooter

Safety considerations aside, mopeds, scooters and motorbikes are almost ideal for the islands in the summer. It almost never rains and what could be more pleasant than a gentle thyme-scented breeze freshening your journey over the mountains? Mopeds are both more economical and more practical than cars. They can fit into almost any boat and travel paths where cars fear to tread. Many islands have scooter rentals which are not expensive, and include third party coverage in most cases. To hire mopeds of under 125cc, you usually just have to leave your passport as security. For larger motorbikes of over 125cc, you must also show a valid car driving licence. For the largest motorbikes (over 250cc) you will need to show a full motorbike licence—assuming that you can find a large motorbike for hire. Most of those smart-looking, 'born-to-be-wild' bikes on display outside hire shops belong to the staff and are left there as lures; they are not for hire. Check the mechanical condition of the bike you're hiring; they are often badly maintained and only given a cursory check between customers. It pays to hire early in the day, because the oldest and ropiest machines will be hired out last.

Be warned that **moped accidents** are one of the most common ways that tourists get injuries in Greece—just look around the beach for evidence of grazed knees, scuffed elbows and legs in plaster, and they're the ones that were lucky. Greece has the second-worst road accident statistics in Europe (after Portugal), and Greek driving skills are not all they should be. So be very, very careful if you're not an experienced motorcyclist. Make sure your **travel insurance** policy covers moped accidents before you go on holiday—many policies exclude mopeds, or include them under additional cover—and try and avoid damaging the bike too, because the 'insurance' hire places offer is barely more than the legal minimum of third-party, and you'll be expected to pay for any damage more extensive than a puncture. Many British tour operators won't insure you for mopeds at all.

By Bicycle

Cycling has not caught on in Greece, either as a sport or as a means of transport, though you can usually hire a cheap (and badly-maintained) mountain bike in most major resorts. If you can put up with an ill-fitting bike with gears that crash and brakes that squeal, they can be a pleasant enough way to get around on short journeys. If you're a keen cyclist, it's a much better idea to take your own bike with you. Check with your airline before flying; the usual stipulations apply, i.e. cover your bike with a cardboard 'bike box' (free from your local bike shop), turn the handlebars, take the pedals out (to prevent them from damaging other luggage), and let the tyre pressures down to half the usual pressure (to prevent the inner tubes exploding at altitude). There is seldom any charge for carrying a bike on a plane, though you may be surcharged if the bike and your other luggage exceed the usual weight limit (most of the time bemused airline staff turn a blind eye). Trains in Greece carry bicycles for a small fee, and Greek boats generally take them along, for nothing. The Ionians islands offer easy riding, but Crete and Evia are the best islands for serious cyclists, Crete being the more rugged by far; mountain bikes are a better choice for island roads than narrow-tyred racing and touring bikes. On the islands you will find fresh water, places to camp, and a warm and surprised welcome in the villages. Make sure both you and your bike have comprehensive accident insurance before you go.

Hitch-Hiking

With the rarest of exceptions, hitch-hiking, or 'autostop' as it is known in Greece, is perfectly safe and common practice on the islands and remote villages. However, the lack of cars makes it a not particularly speedy mode of transport. The Greek double standard produces the following percentages for hopeful hitch-hikers:

Single woman: 99% of cars will stop. You hardly have to stick out your hand. But be careful. Go for a car with a family or couple, and avoid single male drivers to be on the safe side.

Two women: 75% of cars will find room for you.

Woman and man: 50%; more if the woman is pretty.

Single man: 25% if you are well dressed with little luggage; less otherwise.

Two men: start walking.

The best time for soliciting a ride is when you disembark from a ship. Ask your fellow passengers, or better still write your destination on a piece of paper (in Greek if possible) and pin it to your shirt with a naïve and friendly smile. What you lose in dignity you will generally gain in a lift. Strictly speaking hitching is illegal in Greece (though tolerated), so don't be offended if a truck driver sets you and your conspicuous backpack down just before a police checkpoint.

Specialist Holidays

A list of tour operators including specialist ones is available from the:

National Tourist Organization of Greece, ✆ (071) 734 5997 (London), (212) 421 5777 (New York), (312) 782 1084 (Chicago), (213) 6266696 (Los Angeles).

American School of Classical Studies at Athens, 41E 72 St, New York, NY 10021. Offers archaeological tours organized from the USA.

℅ (212) 861 0302 (New York)

Explore Worldwide, 1 Frederick Street, Aldershot, Hants. Walking holidays.

℅ (0252) 344161

Filoxenia Tours, Sourdock Hill, Barkisland, Halifax, West Yorks HX4 0AG. Painting holidays in Kythera (and many other nature and historical holidays in other parts of Greece). They also run OPUS 23, for disabled travellers. ℅ (0422) 375999

Manos Holidays, 168–172 Old Street, London EC1V 9BP. Green beach spring-cleaning weeks on Corfu and Zakynthos. ℅ (071) 216 8000

Peregrine Holidays, 40–41 South Parade, Summertown, Oxford, OX2 7JP. Nature and wildlife tours to the islands, plus Crete and the Peloponnese.

℅ (0865) 511642

Ramblers Holidays, Box 43, Welwyn Garden City, Hertfordshire, AL8 6PQ. Walking holidays with emphasis on archaeology and wildflowers.

℅ (0707) 331133

Waymark Holidays, 44 Windsor Road, Slough, SL1 2EJ. Walking holidays.

℅ (0753) 516477

Customs and Immigration

The formalities for foreign tourists entering Greece are very simple. **American, Australian** and **Canadian** citizens can stay for up to three months in Greece simply on presentation of a valid passport. However, unless you are entering with a car, immigration officials no longer stamp EC passports. **South Africans** are permitted 2 months.

If you want to extend your stay in Greece, you must report to the police 10 days before your visa runs out. (If you are staying in Athens, register at the **Athens Alien Dept**, 173 Alexandras Ave, 115 22 Athens, ℅ (01) 646 8103). Take your passport, four photographs, and bank exchange receipts. The rules vary from province to province, but you will most likely receive a slip of paper authorizing you to stay for a period of up to 6 months; this will cost you 11,000 dr. This has to be renewed at the end of every 6 successive months that you remain in Greece.

If you are about to visit Turkish-occupied North Cyprus, make sure the Turkish authorities stamp a removeable piece of paper in your passport; visitors to North Cyprus since the Turkish occupation are not allowed re-entry to Greece.

One of the great thrills of sailing the Greek waters is the variety of places to visit in a relatively short time, with the bonus that nowhere in Greece is far from safe shelter or harbours with good facilities for yachtsmen. There is little shallow water, except close to the shoreline, few currents and no tides or fog. The 100,000 miles of coastline, and a collection of 3,000 islands and islets, provide a virtually inexhaustible supply of secluded coves and empty beaches, even at the height of the tourist season. Equally, there are berthing facilities in the most popular of international hotspots—it's all there beneath the blue skies and bright sunshine. The Greek National Tourist Organization has initiated a programme of rapid expansion in the face of mounting competition from Turkey and Spain; facilities are being improved and new marinas are being constructed throughout the country.

Greek weather guarantees near-perfect sailing conditions, the only real problem being the strong winds in parts of the country at certain times of the year, notably April to October.

The Ionian Sea and the west coast of the Peloponnese are affected by the *maistros*, a light-to-moderate northwest wind which presents itself in the afternoon only. Less frequently there are westerly winds, from moderate to strong, to the west and south of the Peloponnese. To the south of Attica, and east of the Peloponnese, the sea is to a great extent sheltered by land masses and it is not until summer that the menacing *meltemi* blows.

The Aegean Sea is affected by a northwest wind in the south, and a northeasterly in the north, and when the *meltemi* blows in August and September, it can reach force eight, testing all your skills at the helm. The Turkish coast has light, variable breezes, which are rudely interrupted by the forceful *meltemi*.

This chart shows average wind speeds (in knots) and direction during the months April to October.

Area	Apr	May	Jun	Jul	Aug	Sep	Oct
N.E. Aegean	NE	NE	NE	NE	NE	NE	NE
(Limnos)	10.2	8.2	8.2	10.2	10.2	10.2	11.4
Thrakiko	NE	NE	NE	NE	NE	NE	NE
(Thassos)	1.4	1.4	1.4	1.4	1.4	1.6	2.3
Kos–Rhodes	WNW	WNW	NW	NW	NW	NW	WNW
(Kos)	13.6	13.0	13.0	13.6	13.6	13.0	11.4
S.W. Aegean	N	SW	N	N	N	N	N
(Milos)	9.0	6.6	6.6	8.6	8.6	8.6	9.8
W. Cretan	SW	NNW	NNW	NNW	N	N	N
(Chania)	5.0	4.4	4.4	4.4	4.1	4.1	3.8
E. Cretan	NW	NW	NW	NW	NW	NW	NW
(Herakleon)	6.6	4.4	6.2	8.2	7.4	6.6	5.8
E. Cretan	NW	NW	NW	NW	NW	NW	NW
(Sitia)	6.6	5.0	7.0	8.6	8.2	6.6	5.0
Kythera	NE	W	W	NE	NE	NE	NE
(Kythera)	9.8	8.2	7.8	7.4	8.2	9.0	10.6
Samos Sea	NW	NW	NW	NW	NW	NW	NW
(Samos)	9.4	7.8	9.4	11.0	10.2	8.6	7.0
W. Karpathion	W	W	W	W	W	W	W
(Karpathos)	6.6	6.2	8.6	10.6	9.4	8.2	6.2
N. Ionian	SE	W/SE	W	NW/W	NW	SE	SE
(Corfu)	2.9	2.6	2.9	2.6	2.6	2.3	2.6
N.Ionian	NW	NW	NW	NW	NW	NW/N	NW/NE
(Argostoli)	5.8	5.0	5.4	5.8	5.4	4.4	5.0
S. Ionian	N	NEN	NE	N	NNE	N	NE
(Zakynthos)	9.8	9.4	9.8	10.2	9.8	9.0	10.2
S.Ionian	W	W	W	W	W	W	NE
(Methoni)	11.8	11.0	11.4	11.8	11.0	10.2	9.8

If you wish to skipper a yacht anywhere within the Greek seas, you must consult the *Compile Index Chart of Greek Seas,* otherwise known as *XEE,* published by the Hellenic Navy Hydrographic Service. Basically it is a map of Greece divided into red squares, each with an index number, from which you can select the appropriate charts and order them accordingly (cost approx. 1500 dr.). For non-Greeks, 2500 dr. will buy you what is known as *XEE* 64, a booklet of abbreviations explaining the signs on the charts, with texts in English and Greek.

You also need one of the Pilot series books, which cost 2500 dr. each and cover the following areas in great detail:

Pilot A:	South Albania to Kythera; Ionian Sea, Corinthian Gulf and North Peloponnese shores.
Pilot B:	Southeastern Greek shores; Crete, Eastern Peloponnese, Saronic Gulf and Cyclades.
Pilot C:	Northeastern Greek shores; Evoikos, Pagassitikos, Sporades, Thermaikos, Chalkidiki.
Pilot D:	North and Eastern Aegean shores; Eastern Macedonia, Thrace, Limnos, Lesbos, Chios, Samos, the Dodecanese and Asia Minor.

These describe geographical data, possible dangers, and the present state of transportation and communication. All ports and marinas are mentioned, including where to obtain fresh water and fuel, and there are descriptions of visible inland features. The Hydrographic Service constantly updates the books and sends additional booklets to authorized sellers and to all port authorities, where you may consult them. The nautical charts are updated using the latest most sophisticated methods, and follow standardized dimensions. They are on a 1:100,000 scale for bigger areas and 1:750,000 for ports. Heights and depths are given in metres with functional conversion tables for feet and fathoms.

Further information is provided in booklets called *Notes to Mariners,* published monthly and available for consultation at port authorities. These give information on any alterations to naval charts you have purchased for your voyage. Besides all this there is the Navtex service. A special department of the Hydrographic Service keeps you informed about the weather or any special warnings for the day, through telex, or Navtex. The text is in Greek and English, and there are four retransmission coastal stations covering the Greek seas. Weather forecasts for yachtsmen are broadcast at intervals throughout the day on VHF Channel 16 (in Greek and English); security warnings are also broadcast on this channel, e.g. dangerous wrecks, lights not in operation, etc.

These are some of the ports where fuelling facilities and provisions may be obtained:

Argostoli (Kefalonia)*, Corfu Port*, Gythion*, Chania (Crete)*, Igoumenitsa, Kalamata*, Kapsali (Kythera), Korinthos*, Lefkas, Limeni (Mani), Monemvasia, Nafplion*, Preveza*, Vathi (Ithaca)*, Vouliagmeni Marina, Zakynthos*.

* indicates official ports of entry and exit, where there are port, customs and health authorities, as well as immigration and currency control services.

Main Port Authorities

Piraeus:	(01) 451 1311
Corfu:	(0661) 39918
Herakleon:	(081) 244912
Patras:	(061) 341024

Yachts entering Greek waters must fly the code flag 'Q' until cleared by entry port authorities. Upon arrival the **port authority** (*Limenarkion*) issues all yachts with a transit log, which entitles the yacht and crew to unlimited travel in Greek waters. It also allows crew members to buy fuel, alcohol and cigarettes duty free. It must be kept on board and produced when required, and returned to the customs authorities on leaving Greece at one of the exit ports. Permission is normally given for a stay of 6 months, but this can be extended. Small motor, sail or rowing boats do not require a 'carnet de passage', and are allowed into Greece duty free for 4 months. They are entered in your passport and deleted on exit. For more information, apply to the Greek National Tourist Organisation, 4 Conduit Street, London, W1R 0DJ, ✆ (071) 734 5997, who produce a useful leaflet *Sailing the Greek Seas*.

Anyone taking a yacht by road is strongly advised to obtain boat registration documentation from the DVLA, Swansea, SA99 1BX, ✆ (0792) 783355. The **Royal Yachting Association**, R.Y.A. House, Romsey Road, Eastleigh, Hampshire, SO5 4YA, ✆ (0703) 629962, is a useful source of information.

Monthly Mooring Rates (dr.)

In Alimos Marina (Athens)	*summer*	*winter*
Up to 7m	3300	2800
8–17m	3600	2900
18m and above	3700	3000

Gouvia Marina (Corfu)

Up to 7m	2000	1700
8–17m	2200	1800
18m and above	2400	1900

Yacht Charter

Chartering yachts is very popular these days, and as the promotional literature says, can be cheaper than staying in a hotel (if you have enough friends or family to share expenses). Between the various firms (the National Tourist Organisation has a list) there are over a thousand vessels currently available in all sizes, with or without a crew (though without a crew—bareboat charter—both the charterer and another member of the party must show proof of seamanship: a sailing certificate or letter of recommendation from a recognized yacht or sailing club). There are various options: motor yachts (without sails), motor sailors (primarily powered by motor, auxiliary sail power) and sailing yachts (with auxiliary motor power). Charters can be arranged through licensed firms of yacht brokers, or by contacting yacht owners directly. The **Yacht Charter Association**, 60 Silverdale, New Milton, Hampshire, BH25 7DE, ✆ (0425) 619004, supplies a list of its recognized yacht charter operators and offers advice on chartering overseas. For more information on chartering in Greece, write to:

The Hellenic Professional Yacht Owners Association, 43 Freatidos St, Zea Marina, 18536 Piraeus.   ✆ 452 6335

Greek Yacht Brokers and Consultants Association, 7 Filellinon St, 105 57 Athens.   ✆ (01)323 0330

Greek Yacht Owners Association, 10 Lekka St, 185 37 Piraeus.
                                                                        ✆ (01) 452 6335

One of the largest and most reputable firms is **Valef**, located at 22 Akti Themistokleous, Piraeus, ✆ (01) 428 1920, fax 413780 (in the USA: 7254 Fir Rd, PO Box 391, Ambler, PA 19002). They have more than 300 craft, accommodating 4–50 people in comfort.

Yacht Charter Operators Based in England

Bareboat yacht charter prices start from around £350–£400 per week for a 31-ft boat in low season and £2,500 for a 48-ft boat in high season. Prices peak during July and August and are lower during the spring and autumn months.

BUOYS Cruising Club, 8 Chase Side, Enfield, Middlesex, EN2 6NF. Offers charters from Athens. ℂ (081) 367 8462

Carefree Sailing Ltd, 122 Pavilion Gardens, Laleham, Middlesex, TW18 1HW. Offers charters from Corfu. ℂ (0784) 462796

Creative Holidays & Cruises, 36 Chalton Street, London, NW1. Offers charters from Piraeus. ℂ (071) 383 4243

Marinair, 188 Northdown Road, Cliftonville, Kent, CT9 2QN. Offers charters from Corfu and Athens. ℂ (0843) 227140

McCulloch Marine, 60 Fordwych Road, London, NW2 3TH. Offers charters from Athens. ℂ (081) 452 7509

World Expeditions Ltd, 8 College Rise, Maidenhead, Berkshire, SL6 6BP. From Athens and a number of Greek islands. ℂ (0628) 74174

A number of English-based flotilla companies offer one or two-week sailing holidays, the airfare being included in the total cost. High season prices for a fortnight's holiday range from £550 per person to £1000 per person, depending on the number of people per yacht; expensive enough, but much cheaper than a yacht charter. The yachts have 4–6 berths, are supervized by a lead boat, with experienced skipper, engineer and hostess. Flotilla companies based in England include:

MedChoice, 150 Regent St, London W1R 5FA. ℂ (071) 439 7233

Odysseus Yachting Holidays, 33 Grand Parade, Brighton, BN2 2QA.
ℂ (0273) 695094

Sovereign Sailing, Astral Towers, Betts Way, Crawley, West Sussex RH10 2GX.
ℂ (0293) 599944

Practical A–Z

Average Daily Temperatures

	ATHENS	CRETE (HERAKLEON)	CYCLADES (MYKONOS)	DODECS (RHODES)	IONIAN (CORFU)	N.E. AEGEAN (MYTILINI)	SARONIC (HYDRA)	SPORADES (SKYROS)
	F° C°	F° C°	F° C°	F° C°	F° C°	F° C°	F° C°	F° C°
JAN	48 11	54 12	54 12	54 12	50 10	50 10	53 12	51 10
FEB	49 11	54 12	54 12	54 13	51 10	48 10	53 12	51 10
MAR	54 12	58 14	56 13	58 14	52 12	52 12	56 13	52 11
APR	60 16	62 17	60 17	60 17	60 15	60 16	61 16	58 15
MAY	68 20	68 20	68 20	66 20	66 19	68 20	68 20	66 19
JUN	76 25	74 24	74 23	73 21	71 21	74 24	76 25	74 23
JUL	82 28	78 26	76 25	78 27	78 27	80 27	82 28	77 25
AUG	82 28	78 26	76 25	79 27	78 26	80 27	81 28	78 25
SEP	76 25	76 24	74 23	78 25	74 23	74 23	76 25	71 22
OCT	66 19	70 21	68 20	72 21	66 19	66 19	71 21	65 19
NOV	58 15	64 18	62 17	66 17	58 15	58 15	62 17	58 15
DEC	52 12	58 14	58 14	58 14	54 12	52 12	58 15	51 12

Two Greek measurements you may come across are the *stremma*, a Greek land measurement (1 stremma = ¼ acre), and the *oka*, an old-fashioned weight standard, divided into 400 *drams* (1 *oka* = 3lb; 35 *drams* = ¼lb, 140 *drams* = 1lb).

The **electric current** in Greece is mainly 220 volts, 50Hz; plugs are continental two-pin.

Greek time is Eastern European, or 2 hours ahead of Greenwich Mean Time.

Embassies and Consulates

Australia	37 D. Soutsou St, 115 21 Athens, ℂ 644 7303
Austria	26 Leof. Alexandras, 106 83 Athens, ℂ 821 1036
Canada	4 I. Gennadiou St, 115 21 Athens, ℂ 723 9511
France	7 Vass. Sofias, 106 71 Athens, ℂ 361 1665
Germany	10 Vass. Sofias, 151 24 Athens, ℂ 369 4111
Ireland	7 Vass. Konstantinou, 106 74 Athens, ℂ 723 2771

Japan	Athens Twr., 2–4 Messogion St, 115 27 Athens, ✆ 775 8101
New Zealand	15–17 Tsoha Street, Athens, ✆ 641 0311–5
South Africa	124 Kifissias & Iatridou, 115 10 Athens, ✆ 692 2125
United Kingdom	1 Ploutarchou St, 106 75 Athens, ✆ 723 6211
USA	91 Vass. Sofias, 115 21 Athens, ✆ 721 2951
United Nations	36 Amalias Ave, Athens, ✆ 322 9624

Food and Drink

Eating Out

Eating establishments in Greece are categorized into Luxury, A, B, and C classes. Prices are controlled by the Tourist Police, who also enforce sanitary and health regulations.

The menu in Luxury restaurants is often 'international', with little to reveal that you're in Greece; in others you will find the more basic and authentic Greek cuisine. This is steeped in rich golden olive oil and the ingredients are fresh and often produced locally. It is quite usual in all but the snootiest eating places to examine the dishes (on display behind glass, or in the kitchen) before making a choice. There is usually a menu posted on the door with an English translation, listing the prices, but it's better still to see what the dish of the day is. The availability and variety of fish depends on the catch. Sadly, seafood has become one of the most expensive meals you can order. A combination of increased demand, marketing to Athens, and greedy, unsound fishing practices (such as illegal dynamiting) has decreased the fish population in the Mediterranean, so that what was once common and cheap is now costly and in some places quite rare. Each type of fish has its own price, then your portion is costed by its weight. Restaurants which specialize in fish are called *psarotavernas*.

Pork has taken the place of lamb as the most common meat in Greek tavernas since the country joined the European Community. Almost all *souvlaki* (the ubiquitous chunks of meat grilled on a stick) you get these days is pork, though lamb, roasted or stewed, is still widely available. Beef and chicken are often stewed in a sauce of tomatoes and olive oil, or roasted, accompanied by potatoes, spaghetti or rice. Village feasts, or *paniyiri*, often feature wild goat meat with rice or potatoes. A Greek salad can be just tomatoes or just cucumbers, or village-style *horiatiki* with tomatoes, cucumbers, black olives, peppers, onions and *feta* cheese—a small one for one person and a big one for two or three. You eat this during the meal, dipping your bread in the olive oil. Desserts are not generally eaten in Greece, but in the summer dinner is generally followed by melon or watermelon.

Restaurants (*estiatórion*) serve baked dishes and often grills as well. Restaurants serving just a grill and roasts are called *psistariá*. *Tavernas* may serve baked dishes or a grill or both, and is less formal than a restaurant. Don't be alarmed if food arrives tepid; Greeks believe this is better for the digestion. A sweet shop, or *zacharoplasteíon,* offers honey pastries, cakes, puddings and drinks and sometimes home-made ice cream. Many also serve breakfast, along with the less common dairy shops, or *galaktopoleíon* which sell milk, coffee, bread, yoghurt, rice pudding and custard pies. Cheese pastries (*tyropitta*) and 'tost' can appear almost anywhere. Lager beer is now common in most restaurants, Amstel and Heineken being the most popular, and wine is popular with most meals.

Prices on Greek menus are written first without, then with, service and tax charges. If you are served by a young boy (*mikró*), give him something or leave it on the table—tips are generally all he earns. If you've been given special service, you may leave a tip for your waiter on the plate. The amount varies; up to 10% is quite sufficient in most places.

Wine

The best-known wine of Greece, *retsina*, has a very distinctive taste of pine resin, dating from the time when Greeks stored their wine in untreated pine casks. It is an acquired taste, and many people can be put off by the pungent odour and sharp taste of some bottled varieties. Modern retsinas show increasingly restrained use of resin; all retsinas are best appreciated well-chilled. Draught retsina (*retsina varelisio*) can be found only on some islands, but in Athens it is the accepted, delicious accompaniment to the meal.

Any taverna worth its salt will serve it, and if it's not available you're in the wrong place, unless you've chosen a foreign or fairly exclusive Greek restaurant. In cases of desperation, where no barrelled retsina is on offer, the wine house Kourtakis produces a very acceptable bottled version at a low price. Retsina is admirably suited to Greek food, and after a while a visitor may find non-resinated wines a rather bland alternative. Traditionally it is served in small tumblers, and etiquette requires that they are never filled to the brim or drained empty; you keep topping up your colleagues' glasses, as best you can. There is a great deal of toasting throughout the meal (*stin yamas*—to our health, *stin yassas*—to your health), and by all means clink glasses with someone else, but on no account bring your glass down on another person's (unless your intentions for the evening are entirely dishonourable).

Ordinary red and white house wines are often great locally-produced bargains – *krasi varelisio* or *krasi heema*, *krasi* meaning wine, *varelisio* from the barrel; *heema*, means 'loose'. The customary way of serving these is in small, copper-anodized jugs, in various metric measures (500ml and 250ml being the most common; a standard wine bottle holds 750cl). These are generally fine, though you may be unlucky and get a stinker.

Greece has an ample selection of medium-priced red and white wines, often highly regionalized with each island and village offering their own unique wines. There are many indigenous Greek grape varieties which avoid the tyranny of Cabernet Sauvignon and Chardonnay. All the principal wine companies— Boutari, Achaia-Clauss, Carras, Tsantali, Kourtaki—produce acceptable table wines at very affordable prices. These large Greek wine producers have been investing heavily in new equipment and foreign expertise over the last decade, and it shows; even that humblest of bottles (and Greece's best-seller) *Demestika* has become very acceptable of late, and bears little resemblance to the rough stuff that earned it some unflattering, sound-alike nicknames. Look out for the nobler labels: Boutari *Naoussa* is an old-style, slightly astringent red, while Boutari's *Grande Réserve* is their best red; *Lac des Roches* is their most popular white on the islands. *Peloponnesiakos* from Achaia-Clauss is an easy-drinking, light white wine which is faddishly popular at the moment anywhere within exportable distance of the Peloponnese. From Carras, *Château Carras* is a Bordeaux-style red wine made from the Cabernet Sauvignon and Merlot grapes; if you're lucky you might find *Carras Limnio* a good dinner wine. Boutari's *Santorini* is their finest island white, while in Rhodes in the Dodecanese, CAIR supplies Greece with its sparkling *méthode traditionelle* white, *Caïr*. Emery produces some good whites including Villare.

In recent years small wine producers have become very fashionable with the wine-drinking elite of Greece. Some of these island wine-makers are superb, such as the Gentilini wines produced on Kefalonia; others deserve obscurity. But for the most part, you are unlikely to come across them in the average taverna. If you're a wine buff, it's worth seeking them out from local recommendations in off-licences and high-class restaurants; or better still, consult Maggie McNie of the Greek Wine Bureau in London (071) 823 3799, who is a Master of Wine and probably the best-qualified expert on Greek wines; she can tell you what to try, or what to bring back with you.

Cafés

Cafés or *kafeneíons* (in small towns these are frequented almost exclusively by men, who discuss the latest news, and play cards or backgammon) serve Greek coffee (*café hellinikó*), which is the same stuff as Turkish coffee. There are 40 different ways to make this, although *glykó* (sweet), *métrio* (medium) and *skéto* (no sugar) are the basic orders. It is always served with a glass of water. Nescafé with milk has by popular tourist demand become available everywhere, though Greeks prefer it iced, with or without sugar and milk, which they call *frappé*. Soft drinks and *ouzo* round out the average café fare. Ouzo—like its Cretan cousin *raki*—is a clear anise-flavoured aperitif which many dilute (and cloud) with water. It can be served with a little plate of snacks called *mezédes* which can range from grilled octopus through nuts to cheese and tomatoes, though these days you must request mezédes specially in tourist areas. Brandy, or Metaxa (the Greeks know it by the most popular brand name), is usually a late-night treat. The more stars on the label (from three to seven) the higher the price, and in theory at least, the better the quality. In tourist haunts, milkshakes, fruit juices, cocktails and even capuccino are readily available; in the backwaters you can usually get ice cream and good Greek yoghurt.

Bars

In the last few years the influx of tourists has resulted in the growth of trendy bars, usually playing the latest hit records and serving fancy cocktails as well as standard drinks. These establishments come to life later in the evening, when everyone has spent the day on the beach and the earlier part of the evening in a taverna. They close at 3 or 4am, although amid protest, the Greek Government plans to make this 2am (the Goverment claims the nation is nodding off at work after a night on the tiles). In general they're not cheap, sometimes outrageously dear by Greek standards, and it can be disconcerting to realize that you have paid the same for your Harvey Wallbanger as you paid for the entire meal of chicken and chips, salad and a bottle of wine, half an hour before in the taverna next door. Cocktails have now risen to beyond the 1000 dr. mark in many bars, but before you complain remember that the measures are triples by British standards. If in doubt stick to beer, ouzo, wine and Metaxa (Metaxa and coke, if you can stomach it, is generally about half the price of the better-known Bacardi and coke). You may have difficulty in finding beer, as the profit margin is so small that many bars stop serving it in the peak season, thus obliging you to plump for the higher-priced drinks. One unfortunate practice on the islands is the doctoring of bottles, whereby some bar owners buy cheaper versions of spirits and use them to refill brand name bottles. The only way to be sure is to see the new bottle being opened in front of you.

A list of items which appear frequently on Greek menus is included in the language section at the end of the guide.

Health

In theory there is at least one doctor (*iatrós*) on every island, whose office is open from 9am to 1pm and from 5pm to 7pm. On many islands too there are hospitals which are open all day, and usually have an outpatient clinic, open in the mornings. British travellers are often urged to carry a **Form E111**, available from DSS offices (apply well in advance on a form CM1 from post offices), which admit them to the most basic IKA (Greek NHS) hospitals for treatment; but this doesn't cover medicines or nursing care, which still have to be paid for. In any case, the E111 seems to be looked on with total disregard outside of Athens. Private doctors and hospital stays can be very expensive, so you should take out a **travel insurance** policy, then claim your money back on return to the UK. Greek General Practitioners' fees are, however, usually reasonable.

If you have a serious injury or illness, consider leaving Greece for treatment back home if you are well enough to travel, because even the best hospitals (in Athens) lag many years behind northern Europe or the USA in the modernity of their methods of care and treatment. It's common for families to bring food in for the patient. So make sure your holiday insurance also has adequate repatriation cover.

Most doctors pride themselves on their English, as do their friends the pharmacists (found in the *farmakeio*), whose advice on minor ailments is good, although their medicine is not particularly cheap. If you forgot to bring your own condoms and are caught short, they are widely available from *farmakeio* and even kiosks, with lusty brand names such as 'Squirrel' or 'Rabbit'. If you can't see them on display, the word *kapotes* (condom) gets results. You can also get the Pill, *xapi antisiliptiko*, morning-after Pill and HRT over the pharmacy counter without a prescription. Be sure to take your old packet to show them the brand you use.

A few hints: Coca Cola or retsina reduces the impact of the oil in Greek foods. Fresh parsley can also help stomach upsets.

Money

The word for bank in Greek is *trápeza*, derived from the word *trapezi*, or table, used back in the days of money changers. On all the islands with more than goats and a few shepherds there is some sort of banking establishment. If you plan to spend time on one of the more remote islands, however, such as Antikythera or Kastellorizo, it is safest to bring enough drachma with you. On the other hand, the small but popular islands often have only one bank, where exchanging money can take a long time. Waiting can be avoided if you go at 8am, when the banks open (normal banking hours are 8–2, 8–1 on Fri). Most island banks are closed on Saturdays and Sundays. Better still, post offices will exchange cash, travellers's cheques and Eurocheques; they also charge less commission than banks, and the queues are usually shorter. The number of 24-hour automatic cash tellers are growing in Athens and large resorts such as Corfu Town.

Credit cards can be used to withdraw cash at banks; put your account into credit before going abroad, and this will often be the cheapest way to transfer money. The Commerical Bank of Greece will allow you to withdraw money by Visa, and the National Bank of Greece will exchange on Access (MasterCard). Money can also be withdrawn from some automatic tellers (24 hours daily).

Bank cards There are increasing numbers of cash dispensers for Eurocheque cards, Cirrus and Plus cards in Athens and the big tourist resorts.

Eurocheques are accepted in banks and post offices.

Traveller's cheques are always useful even though commission rates are less for cash. The major brands of traveller's cheques (Thomas Cook and American

Express) are accepted in all banks and post offices; take your passport as ID, and shop around for commission rates.

Running out? Athens and Piraeus, with offices of many British and American banks, are the easiest places to have money sent by cash transfer from someone at home if you run out—though it may take a few days. If there's no bank on the island you're on, the shipping agent will change money, and the post office will change Eurocheques.

The **Greek drachma** is circulated in coins of 100, 50, 20, 10, 5, 2 and 1 drachma and in notes of 100, 500, 1000 and 5000 drachma.

Museums

All significant archaeological sites and museums have regular admission hours. Nearly all are closed on Mondays, and open other weekdays from 8 or 9am to around 2pm, though outdoor sites tend to stay open later, until 4 or 5pm. As a rule, plan to visit cultural sites in the mornings to avoid disappointment, or unless the local tourist office can provide you with current opening times. Hours tend to be shorter in the winter. Students with a valid identification card get a discount on admission fees; on Sundays admission is generally free for EC nationals.

If you're currently studying archaeology, the history of art or the Classics and intend to visit many museums and sites in Greece, it may be worth your while to obtain a free pass by writing several weeks in advance of your trip to the Museum Section, Ministry of Science and Culture, Aristidou 14, Athens, enclosing verification of your studies from your college or university. Entrance fees for sites or museums are not listed in this book. Count on 400–600 dr. in most cases; exceptions are the Acropolis and National Archaeology Museum in Athens at 1500 dr.

Music and Dancing

Greek music is either city music or village music. The music of the city includes the popular tunes, *rembetika* (derived from the hashish dens of Asia Minor) and most bouzouki music. Village music means traditional tunes played on the Greek bagpipes (*tsamboúna*), the clarinet (*klaríno*), the violin and sometimes the dulcimer (*sandoúri*). Cretan music specializes in the lyre (*lyra*) and is in a category of its own.

On the islands you can hear both city and village music, the former at the *bouzoukia*, or Greek nightclubs, which usually feature certain singers. Many play records or washed-out muzak until midnight as the customers slowly arrive. Smaller, rougher night clubs are called *boites* or *skilakia* —'dog' shops. You generally buy a bottle of white wine and fruit and dance until four in the morning, though expect to pay a pretty drachma for the privilege. To hear traditional music, you must go into the villages, to the festivals or weddings. In many places Sunday evening is an occasion for song and dance. Village music is generally modest and unpretentious, while city music is the domain of the professional singers, although any bold member of the audience with a good voice can get up to sing a few songs. After a few hours of drinking, a particular favourite or a good dancer is liable to make the enthusiasts forget the law against *spásimo*, or plate breaking, and supporters may end up paying for missing place settings. If the mood really heats up, men will dance with wine glasses or bottles on their heads, or even sink their teeth into a fully-set table and dance without spilling a drop. When the matrons begin to belly-dance on the table, you know it's time to leave.

In the tavernas you're liable to hear either city or village music. Some put on permanent shows, and others have music only occasionally. Athens is awash with tourist shows and discotheques during the summer but starts pulsating to all kinds of Greek music in November, when Plaka is returned to the Athenians. Most musicians on the islands go to Athens in the winter.

The lyrics to most Greek songs deal with the ups and downs of love; *s'agapoh* means 'I love you'. Serious composers (Mikis Theodorakis is the best known) often put poetry to music, providing splendid renderings of the lyrics of George Seferis and Yannis Ritsos. The guerrillas (*partizanis*) and the Communists have a monopoly on the best political songs, many by Theodorakis. Cretan songs are often very patriotic (for Crete) and many are drawn from the 17th-century epic poem, the *Erotókritos*, written in the Cretan dialect by Vitzentzios Kornáros.

Every island in Greece has its special dance, although today it is often only the young people's folkdance societies that keep them alive, along with the island's traditional costumes. The best time to find them dancing is on each island's Day of Liberation from the Turks or any other anniversary of local significance. One of the best-known professional folkdance companies, based in Athens is:

> **Dora Stratou Greek Folk Dances**, Dora Stratou Theatre, Philopappou Hill, Athens © 324 4395 or © 921 4650. From beginning of May to end of September. Shows begin at 10pm every day, with an additional show at 8pm on Wednesdays and Sundays. Tickets average 1200 dr.; 700 dr. for students.

Although these shows are beautiful and interesting, there's nothing like getting up to dance yourself—a splendid way to work off the big dinner just consumed at a *paniyiri*. For a brief overview of the most popular dances, *see* p. 63.

National Holidays

Note that most businesses and shops close down for the afternoon before and the morning after a religious holiday. If a national holiday falls on a Sunday, the following Monday is observed. The Orthodox Easter is generally a week or so after the Roman Easter.

1 January	New Year's Day	*Protochroniá;* also *Aghios Vassilis* (Greek Father Xmas)
6 January	Epiphany	*Ta Fórce/Epifania*
circa 14 March	'Clean Monday' (precedes Shrove Tuesday, and follows a three-week carnival)	*Kathari Deftéra*
25 March	Greek Independence Day	*Evangelismós*
circa 29 April	Good Friday	*Megáli Paraskevi*
circa 1 May	Easter Sunday	*Páscha*
circa 2 May	Easter Monday	*Theftéra tou Páscha*
circa 3 May	Labour Day	*Protomaya*
15 August	Assumption of the Virgin	*Koímisis tis Theotókou*
28 October	'Ochi' Day (in celebration of Metaxas' 'no' to Mussolini)	
25 December	Christmas	*Christoúyena*
26 December	Gathering of the Virgin	*Sinaxi Theotóku*

In Greece, Easter is the big national holiday, the equivalent of Christmas and New Year in northern climes and the time of year when far-flung relatives return to Greece to see their families back home; it's a good time of year to visit for atmosphere, with fireworks and feasting. After the priest has intoned: *'O Christos Aneste!'*—Christ has risen!—families return home with lighted candles, mark the sign of the cross on the doorpost, and tuck into a special meal of *mayaritsa* soup. On Easter Sunday the Paschal lamb is spit-roasted and music and dancing goes on day and night. After Easter and May 1, spring (*anixi*—the opening) has offically come, and the tourist season begins.

Festival dates for saints' days vary over a period of several given days, or even weeks, due to the Greek liturgical calendar; we have given the 1994 dates when known, but check these locally, if you can, for following years.

Packing

Even in the height of summer, evenings can be chilly in Greece, especially when the *meltemi* wind is blowing. Always bring at least **one warm sweater** and a pair of long trousers. Those who venture off the beaten track into the thorns and rocks should bring sturdy and comfortable shoes—trainers (sneakers) are good. Cover the ankles if you really like wilderness, where scorpions and harmful snakes can be a problem. Plastic flip-flops are recommended for rocky beaches, where there are often sea urchins; you can easily buy them near any beach if you don't want to carry them around with you.

Summer travellers following whim rather than a pre-determined programme should bring a **sleeping bag**, as lodgings of any sort are often full to capacity. Serious sleeping-baggers should also bring a Karrimat or similar insulating layer to cushion them from the gravelly Greek ground. Torches are very handy for moonless nights, caves and rural villages.

On the pharmaceutical side, **seasickness pills**, insect bite remedies, tablets for stomach upsets and aspirin will deal with most difficulties encountered. Women's sanitary towels and sometimes Tampax are sold from general stores, but on remote islands you'll need to seek out the *farmakeio;* if there's no pharmacy, you've had it. Soap, washing powder, a clothes line and especially a towel are necessary for those staying in class C hotels or less. Most important of all, buy a universal-fitting sink plug if you like sinks full of water; Greek sinks rarely have working ones. A knife is a good idea for *paniyiria*, where you are often given a slab of goat meat with only a spoon or fork to eat it with. A photo of the family and home is always appreciated by new Greek friends.

On all the Greek islands except for the most remote of the remote you can buy whatever you forgot to bring. Toilet paper and mosquito coils are the two most common purchases on arrival. However, special needs such as artificial sweeteners, contact lens products and so on can generally be found in Athens and the more popular islands.

Finally let common sense and the maxim 'bring as little as possible and never more than you can carry' dictate your packing; work on the theory that however much money and clothing you *think* you need, you should halve the amount of clothing and double the money.

Photography

Greece lends herself freely to beautiful photography, but a fee is charged at archaeological sites and museums. For a movie camera of any kind, including camcorders, you are encouraged to buy a ticket for the camera; with a tripod you pay per photograph at sites, but cameras (especially tripod-mounted ones) are not allowed in museums, for no particular reason other than the museum maintaining a monopoly on its own (usually very dull) picture stock. 35mm film, both print and slide, can be found in many island shops, though it tends to be expensive and the range of film speeds limited (100ASA and 64ASA are easily available though if you take slides). Disposable and underwater cameras are on sale in larger holiday resorts. Large islands even have 24-hour developing services, though again this costs more than at home.

The light in the summer is often stronger than it seems and is the most common cause of ruined photographs; opting for slow film (100ASA or less) will help. Greeks usually love to have their pictures taken, and although it's more polite to ask first, you should just go ahead and take the photo if you don't want them to rush off to beautify themselves and strike a pose. You should avoid taking pictures of the aircraft, military installations and barracks, communications systems on mountain tops, and Army look-out posts. The Photography Forbidden sign shows a camera with a cross through it and speaks for itself.

If you bring an expensive camera to Greece, it never hurts to insure it. Above all, never leave it alone 'for just a few minutes'. Although Greeks themselves very rarely steal anything, other tourists are not so honest.

Post Offices

Signs for post offices *(tachidromío)* as well as postboxes *(kourti)* are bright yellow and easy to find. Many post office employees speak English. Stamps can also be bought at kiosks and in some tourist shops, although they charge a small commission. Stamps are *grammatósima*. Postcards can take up to three weeks to arrive at their destinations, or only a week if you're lucky; letters sent abroad are faster, taking just over a week, depending on the route. If you're really in a hurry you can send letters *Express* for extra cost.

If you do not have an address, mail can be sent to you *Poste Restante* to any post office in Greece, and can be picked up with proof of identity. After one month all unretrieved letters are returned to sender. If someone has sent you a parcel, you will receive a notice of its arrival, and you must go to the post office to collect it. You will have to pay a handling fee of 650 dr, and customs charges and duties should the parcel contain dutiable articles. 'Fragile' stickers attract scant attetion. In small villages, particularly on the islands, mail is not delivered to the house but to the village centre, either a café or bakery. Its arrival coincides with that of a ship from Athens.

If you want to mail a package, any shop selling paper items will wrap it for a small fee.

Sports

Watersports

Naturally these predominate in the islands. All popular beaches these days hire out pedal boats and windsurf boards; some have paragliding and jet skis. Water-skiing prevails on most islands and large hotel complexes. Several islands offer sailing and windsurfing instruction. For more details contact:

Hellenic Yachting Federation, 7 Akti Navarchou Kountourioti, Piraeus, © 413 7351.

Greek Windsurfing Association, 7 Filellinon St, Piraeus, © 323 3696.

Underwater activities with any kind of breathing apparatus are strictly forbidden to keep divers from snatching any antiquities and to protect marine life. However, snorkelling is fine, and Corfu has a diving school at Paleokastritsa—where, even if you already know how to dive, you have to go out with their boats.

Nudism is forbidden by law in Greece, except in designated areas, such as the more remote beaches of Mykonos in the Cyclades. In practice, however, many people shed all in isolated coves, at the far ends of beaches, or ideally on beaches accessible only by private boat. On the other hand, topless sunbathing is now legal on the majority of popular beaches *away* from settlements. Do exercise discretion. It isn't worth wounding local sensibilities, no matter how prudish other people's attitudes may seem. You could be arrested on the spot and end up with three days in jail or a stiff fine. Canoodling on public beaches in broad daylight can also offend.

Average Sea Temperatures

Jan	Feb	Mar	Apr	May	Jun	Jul	Aug	Sep	Oct	Nov	Dec
59°F	59°F	59°F	61°F	64°F	72°F	75°F	77°F	75°F	72°F	64°F	63°F
15°C	15°C	15°C	16°C	18°C	22°C	24°C	25°C	24°C	22°C	18°C	17°C

36   *Practical A–Z*

Land Sports

Tennis is very popular in Athens with numerous clubs from Glyfada to Kiffissia. There are two on the Ionian islands too, at 4 Romanou St, **Corfu Town**, © 37021, and at **Kefalomandouko**.

Otherwise there are courts at all major resort hotels, where, if you are not a resident, you may be allowed to play in the off season.

The **Corfu Golf Club**, Ropa Valley, P.O. Box 71, © 94220/1, admits non-members. The course has 18 holes, par 72, practice range, equipment hire and shop, changing rooms, and restaurant. Green fees are 7000 dr. daily in May, Sept and Oct, less in other months. Lessons can be had for 4000 dr. per half hour.

Organized **horse riding** is offered at the **Corfu Riding Club**, Kerkira Beach, Gouvia, © 91325. Open Apr–Oct, 7–10am and 5–9pm, though many small riding stables can be found on other islands. In Athens, call the **Riding Club of Greece**, Paradissos, © (01) 682 6128, and the **Riding Club of Athens**, Gerakos, © (01) 661 1088.

Telephones

The *Organismos Telepikoinonia Ellathos*, better known as *OTE*, has offices in the larger towns and at least one on every island that has a telephone service; these are the best place to make international calls. You can call both direct and collect (reverse charges), although the latter usually takes at least half an hour to put through. On the larger islands you may dial abroad direct (for Great Britain dial 0044 and for the USA 001 before the area code). A 3-minute call to the UK will cost about 750 dr., to the US 1600 dr. You should also use OTE for calling other places in Greece. Telegrams can be sent from OTE or the post office.

Payphones don't exist as such; the few that there were have been replaced with cardphones during the summer of 1993. Calls can be made from kiosks (more expensive), *kafeneíos*, and shops (always ask first). Phonecards have now come to Athens and the busier resorts but some islands only have the blue booths without the phones *in situ* yet. Buy a card when you arrive at the airport, or from any *periptero* at 1000 dr. for 100 units or *monades*.

It is often impossible to call Athens from the islands in mid-morning; chances improve in the evening. To defeat the beeps, whirrs, and buzzes you often get instead of a connection, wait for the series of six clicks after the area code is dialled before proceeding.

It's customary in Greece to put the used toilet paper in a special wastebasket beside the toilet (which is emptied regularly); this is a habit left over from the days when toilet paper blocked the inadequate Greek plumbing. However, Greek plumbing has improved remarkably in the past few years, especially in the newer hotels and restaurants. Nevertheless, public toilets and those in cheaper hotels and pensions often have their quirks. **Tavernas**, *kafeneíons*, and **sweet shops** almost always have facilities (it's good manners to buy something before you excuse yourself).

In older pensions and tavernas, the plumbing often makes up in inventiveness for what it lacks in efficiency. Do not tempt fate by disobeying the little notices 'the papers they please to throw in the basket'—or it's bound to lead to trouble. Also, a second flush in immediate succession will gurgle and burp instead of swallow. Many places in Greece have only a ceramic hole. Women who confront this for the first time should take care not to wet their feet: squat about halfway and lean back as far as you can. Always have paper of some sort handy.

If you stay in a private room or pension you may have to have the electric water heater turned on for about 20 minutes before you take a shower, so if you were promised hot water but it fails to appear, ask the proprietor about it. In most smaller *pensions*, water is heated by a solar panel on the roof, so the best time to take a shower is in the late afternoon, or the early evening (before other residents use up the finite supply of hot water). In larger hotels there is often hot water in the mornings and evenings, but not in the afternoons. Actually 'cold' showers in the summer aren't all that bad, because the tap water itself is generally lukewarm, especially after noon. A good many showers are of the hand-held variety; sinks in Greece rarely have plugs.

Greek tap water is perfectly safe to drink. Big plastic bottles of spring water are widely available, even on ships, and taste better than tap water.

Tourist Information

If the **Greek National Tourist Organisation** (in Greek the initials come out: EOT) can't answer your questions about Greece, at least they can refer you to someone who can.

In Athens:

EOT Information Desk: National Bank of Greece, Syntagma Square, 2 Karageorgi Servias St, ℂ (01) 322 2545, 323 4130

EOT, East Airport: ✆ (01) 969 9590.
Head Office: 2 Amerikis St, Athens 10564, ✆ (01) 322 3111; fax 322 2841.

In Australia

51–57 Pitt St, Sydney, NSW 2000, ✆ 241 1663/4; fax 235 2174.

In Canada

1300 Bay St, Toronto, Ontario, ✆ (416) 968 2220, fax 968 6533.
1233 De La Montagne, Montreal, Quebec, ✆ (514) 871 1535, fax 871 1535.

In Great Britain

4 Conduit St, London W1R 0DJ, ✆ (071) 734 5997, fax 287 1369.

In the US

Head Office: Olympic Tower, 645 Fifth Ave, 5th Floor, New York, NY 10022,
✆ (212) 421 5777; fax 826 6940.
168 N. Michigan Ave, Chicago, Ill. 60601, ✆ (312) 782 1084; fax 782 1091.
611 West Sixth St, Suite 2198, Los Angeles, Calif. 90017, ✆ (213) 626 6696; fax
489 9744.

Islands without a branch of the EOT often have some form of local tourist office; if
not, most have **Tourist Police** (often located in an office in the town's police station). You can always tell a Tourist Policeman from other policemen by the little
flags he wears on his pocket, showing which languages he speaks. They have
information about the island, and can often help you find a room. In Athens there
are four Tourist Police stations, and a magic telephone number—171. The voice
on 171 not only speaks good English, but can tell you everything from ship departures to where to spend the night.

Tourist Police in Athens

Dimitrakopoloulou 77, Veikou (the new home of 171).
Larissa Train Station, ✆ 821 3574.
West Airport, Olympic Airways, ✆ 981 4093.
East Airport, ✆ 969 9523.
At **Piraeus** the Tourist Police are on Akti Miaouli, ✆ 452 3670/418
4815.

Travelling with Children

Greece is one of the best Mediterranean countries to bring a child, as children are
not barely tolerated as they are in more 'sophisticated' holiday resorts, but are

generally enjoyed and encouraged. Depending on their age, they go free or receive discounts on ships and buses. You can also save on hotel bills by bringing sleeping bags for the children. However, if they're babies, don't count on island pharmacies stocking your baby's brand of milk powder or baby foods—they may have some, but it's safest to bring your own supply. Disposable nappies, especially Pampers, are widely available, even on the smaller islands. Travelling with a baby is like having a special passport. Greeks adore them, so don't be too surprised if your infant is passed round like a parcel. Greek children usually have an afternoon nap, so do their parents, so it's quite normal for Greeks to eat *en famille* until the small hours. The attitude to children is very different to the British one of being seen but not heard—Greek children are spoiled rotten. Finding a babysitter is never a problem.

Superstitions are still given more than credit than you might expect; even in the most cosmopolitan of households, you'll see babies with amulets pinned to their clothes or wearing blue beads to ward off the evil eye before their baptism. Beware of commenting on a Greek child's intelligence, beauty or whatever, as this may call down the jealous interest of the old gods. The response in the old days was to spit in the admired child's face, but these days, superstitious grannies will say the ritual 'phtew—phtew—phtew', as if spitting, to protect the child from harm.

Where to Stay

Hotels

All hotels in Greece are divided into six categories: Luxury, A, B, C, D and E. This grading system bears little relationship to the quality of service or luxury; it's more to do with how the building is constructed, size of bedrooms, etc. If the hotel has a marble-clad bathroom it gets a higher rating. For this reason, some D and C class hotels can be better than Bs. You may come across government-run hotels, *Xenias*, many of which look like barracks. Some of these are better than others.

Prices are set and strictly controlled by the Tourist Police. Off season you can generally get a discount, sometimes as much as 40%. In the summer season prices can be increased by up to 20%. Other charges include an 8% government tax, a 4.5% community bed tax, a 12% stamp tax, an optional 10% surcharge for stays of only one or two days, an air conditioning surcharge, as well as a 20% surcharge for an extra bed. All of these prices are listed on the door of every room and authorized and checked at regular intervals. If your hotelier fails to abide by the posted prices, or if you have any other reason to believe all is not on the level, take your complaint to the Tourist Police.

1994 hotel rate guideline in drachma for mid-high season (1/5/94–30/9/94)*

	L	A	B	C	D
Single room with bath	9–30,000	6.7–15,000	6.7–10,000	4.5–8000	2.7–5000
Double room with bath	13.1–35,000	9.9–17,000	5.7–14,000	4.6–10,000	4–6000

* 1994 maximum prices were still not confirmed at the time of writing, as the change of Government in late 1993 disabled the civil service and EOT for months; the above prices are based on the most up-to-date information available in Spring 1994.

Prices for E hotels are about 20% less than D rates.

During the summer, hotels with restaurants may require guests to take their meals in the hotel, either full pension or half pension, and there is no refund for an uneaten dinner. Twelve noon is the official check-out time, although on the islands it is usually geared to the arrival of the next boat. Most Luxury and class A, if not B, hotels situated far from the town or port supply buses or cars to pick up guests.

Hotels down to class B all have private bathrooms. In C most do. In D you will be lucky to find a hot shower, and in E forget it. In these hotels neither towel nor soap is supplied, although the bedding is clean.

The importance of reserving a room in advance, especially during July and August, cannot be over-emphasized. Reservations can be made through the individual hotel or the **Hellenic Chamber of Hotels**, 24 Stadiou St, 105 61 Athens, © (01) 323 6962 (from Athens: between 8am and 2pm); fax (01) 322 5449.

In the 'Where to Stay' sections of this book, accommodation is listed according to the following categories. Prices quoted are for **double rooms** (*drachma*).

luxury	15,000 dr. and above
expensive	8–15,000 dr.
moderate	4–8000 dr.
cheap	4000 dr. and below

Rooms (Domatia) in Private Homes

These are for the most part cheaper than hotels and are sometimes more pleasant. On the whole, Greek houses aren't much in comparison to other European homes mainly because the Greeks spend so little time inside them; but they are clean, and the owner will often go out of his or her way to assure maximum comfort for the guest. Staying in someone's house can also offer rare insights into Greek domestic taste, which ranges from a near-Japanese simplicity to a clutter of bulging plastic cat pictures that squeak when you touch them; lamps shaped like ships, made entirely of macaroni; tapestries of dogs shooting pool; and flocked sofas covered in heavy plastic that only the Patriarch of the Orthodox Church is allowed to sit in. Increasingly, however, rooms to rent to tourists are built in a separate annexe and tend to be rather characterless.

While room prices are generally fixed in the summer—the going rate in high season is now 4000 dr.—out of season they are always negotiable (with a little finesse), even in June.

Prices depend a lot on the island and the resort. Speaking some Greek is the biggest asset in bargaining, although not strictly necessary. Claiming to be a poor student is generally effective. Always remember, however, that you are staying in someone's home, and do not waste more water or electricity than you need. The owner will generally give you a bowl to wash your clothes in, and there is always a clothes line.

The Tourist Police on each island have all the information on rooms and will be able to find you one, if you do not meet a chorus of Greeks chanting 'Rooms? Rooms?' as you leave the boat. Many houses also have signs.

Youth Hostels

Some of these are official and require a membership card from the Association of Youth Hostels, or alternatively an International Membership Card (about 2500 dr.) from the Greek Association of Youth Hostels, 4 Dragatsaniou St, Athens, © (01) 323 4107; other hostels are informal, have no irksome regulations, and admit anyone. There are official youth hostels on Corfu. Most charge extra for a shower, sometimes for sheets. Expect to pay 600–1200 dr. a night, depending on the quality of facilities and services offered. The official ones have a curfew around midnight.

Camping Out

The climate of summertime Greece is perfect for sleeping out of doors. Unauthorized camping is illegal in Greece, although each village on each island enforces the ban as it sees fit. Some couldn't care less if you put up a tent at the edge of their beach; in others the police may pull up your tent pegs and fine you. All you can do is ask around to see what other tourists or friendly locals advise. In July and August you only need a sleeping bag to spend a pleasant night on a remote beach, cooled by the sea breezes that also keep hopeful mosquitoes at bay. Naturally, the more remote the beach, the less likely you are to be disturbed. If a policeman does come by and asks you to move, though, you had best do so; be diplomatic. Many islands have privately-operated camping grounds—each seems to have at least one. These are reasonably priced, though some have only minimal facilities. The National Tourist Office controls other, 'official', campsites which are rather plush and costly.

There are three main reasons behind the camping law: one is that the beaches have no sanitation facilities for crowds of campers; secondly, forest fires are a real hazard in summer; and thirdly, the law was enacted to displace gipsy camps, and is still used for this purpose. If the police are in some places lackadaisical about enforcing the camping regulations, they come down hard on anyone lighting any kind of fire in a forest, and may very well put you in jail for 2 months; every year forest fires damage huge swathes of land.

National Tourist Office of Greece **camping rates** per day during high season:

	dr.		
Adult:	600	–	800
Child (4–12):	300	–	500
Caravan:	1000	–	1300
Small tent:	500	–	650
Large tent:	900	–	1200
Car:	150	–	200

Renting a House or Villa

On most islands it is possible to rent houses or villas, generally for a month or more at a time. Villas can often be reserved from abroad: contact a travel agent or the National Tourist Organisation (NTOG) for names and addresses of rental agents. In the off season houses may be found on the spot with a little enquiry; with luck you can find a house sleeping 2–3 people, and depending on the facilities it can work out quite reasonably per person. Corfu has sophisticated villa rentals (i.e. with a large number of purpose-built properties with all the amenities, handled by agents in Athens, Great Britain and North America). The NTOG has a list of agents offering villas and apartments. Facilities normally include a refrigerator, hot water, plates and utensils, etc. Generally, the longer you stay the more economical it is. Things to check for are leaking roofs, creeping damp, water supply (the house may have a well) and a supply of lamps if there is no electricity.

Self-catering Holiday Agents

Airtours, Wavell House, Helmshore, Rossendale, Lancashire, BB4 4NB. Self-catering on Corfu, Zakynthos and Kefalonia. ✆ (0706) 260000

Corfu à la Carte, 8 Deanwood House, Stockcross, Newbury, Berkshire, RG16 8JP. Villas and cottages on Corfu. ✆ (0635) 30621

CV Travel, 43 Cadogan Street, London, SW3 2PR. Villas and apartments on Corfu and Paxos. ✆ (071) 581 0851

Filoxenia Tours, Sourdock Hill, Barkisland, Halifax, West Yorks HX4 0AG. Exclusive tailor-made holidays on the mainland plus Corfu, Kefalonia and Kythera. ✆ (0422) 375999

Greek Islands Club, 66 High Street, Walton-on-Thames, Surrey, KT12 1BU.

Apartments and villas on Corfu, Paxos, Ithaca, Kefalonia and Kythera. ✆ (0932) 220477

Greek Sun Holidays, 1 Bank Street, Sevenoaks, Kent, TN13 1UW. Apartments and studios on Kythera and Paxos. ✆ (0732) 740317

Ilios Island Holidays, 18 Market Square, Horsham, West Sussex, RH12 1E. Villas and apartments on Zakynthos, Lefkas and Kefalonia. ✆ (0403) 59788

Manos Holidays, 168-172 Old Street, London EC1V 9BP. Accommodation in major resorts, plus Lefkas. ✆ (071) 216 8000

Meon Travel, Meon House, College Street, Petersfield, Hampshire, GU32 3JN.

Villas on Corfu and Paxos. ✆ (0730) 268411

Something Special, 10 Bull Plain, Hertford, Hertfordshire, SG14 1DT. Villas and apartments on Corfu. ✆ (0992) 552231

Sunvil Holidays, 7–8 Upper Square, Old Isleworth, Middlesex, TW7 7BJ. Small resorts on Lefkas and Corfu. ✆ (081) 568 4499.

Traditional Settlements in Greece

This is a programme sponsored by the National Tourist Organisation of Greece to preserve old villages and certain buildings while converting their interiors into tourist accommodation with modern amenities. Often these are furnished with handmade furniture and weaving typical of the locale. The aim is to offer visitors a taste of rural life while improving the economy in these areas. So far guesthouses are available on Kefalonia, and in several villages on the mainland; others are planned for the future. Prices are quite reasonable (especially when compared with the going rate for villas) and information may be had by writing to the nearest Greek National Tourist Organisation/EOT. You can then book direct, or through EOT.

Women Travellers

Greece is fine for women travellers but foreign women travelling alone can be viewed as an oddity in some places. Be prepared for a fusillade of questions. Greeks tend to do everything in groups or *pareas* and can't understand people who want to go solo. That said, Greece is a choice destination for women travelling on their own. Out of respect Greeks on the whole refrain from annoying women as other Mediterranean men are known to do, while remaining friendly and easy to meet; all the Greek men from sixteen to sixty like to chat up foreign women, but extreme coercion and violence such as rape is rare. Men who try to take advantage of women or chase tourists are generally looked down on and have bad reputations. While some Greek men can't fathom what sexual equality might mean—they are usually the same who hold the fantasy that for a woman a night without company is unbearable mortification of the flesh—they are ever courteous and will rarely allow even the most liberated female (or male) guest to pay for anything.

In the major resorts like Corfu, tourist women are considered fair game, fish to be harpooned in more ways than one by the local lads throughout the season. A *kamaki* is a harpoon in Greek, and also the name given to the Romeos who usually roar about on motorbikes, hang out in the bars and cafés, and hunt in pairs or packs. Their aim is to collect as many women as possible, notching up points for different nationalities. There are highly professional *kamakis* in the big resorts, gigolos who live off women tourists, gathering as many foreign hearts plus gold chains and parting gifts as they can; they overwinter all over the world with members of their harem. Other Greeks look down on them, and consider them dishonourable and no good.

Many young Greek women are beginning to travel alone—that leggy blonde with the rucksack could just as well be Greek as Swedish nowadays—but this is no indication that traditional values are disappearing. Although many women in the larger towns now have jobs, old marriage customs still exert a strong influence, even in Athens. Weddings are sometimes less a union of love than the closing of a lengthily negotiated business deal. In the evenings, especially at weekends, you'll see many girls of marriageable age join the family for a seaside promenade, or *volta*, sometimes called 'the bride market'. A young man, generally in his late twenties or early thirties, will spot a likely girl on the promenade or will hear about her through the grapevine. He will then approach the father to discover the girl's dowry—low wages and high housing costs demand that it contains some sort of living quarters from the woman's father, often added on top of the family house. The suitor must have a steady job. If both parties are satisfied, the young man is officially introduced to the daughter, who can be as young as 16 in the villages. If they get along well together, the marriage date is set. The woman who never marries and has no children is sincerely pitied in Greece. The inordinate number of Greek widows (and not all wear the traditional black) is due to the traditional 10- to 20-year age difference between husband and wife.

Because foreign men don't observe the Greek customs, their interest in a Greek woman will often be regarded with suspicion by her family. Although the brother probably won't brandish a knife at a man for glancing at his sister, he is likely to tell him to look elsewhere.

Working

If you run out of money in Greece, it usually isn't too difficult to find a temporary job on the islands, ranging from polishing cucumbers to laying cement. The local *kafeneíon* is a good place to enquire. Work on yachts can sometimes be found by asking around at the Athenian marinas. The theatre agents, for work as extras in films, are off Academias Ave, by Kanigos Square. Teachers may apply to one of the seven English/American schools in Athens, or apply as an English teacher to a *frontistirion*, a poorly-paid, private school. The *Athens News*, the country's English daily, and *The Athenian*, a monthly publication, often have classified advertisements for domestic, tutorial, and secretarial jobs.

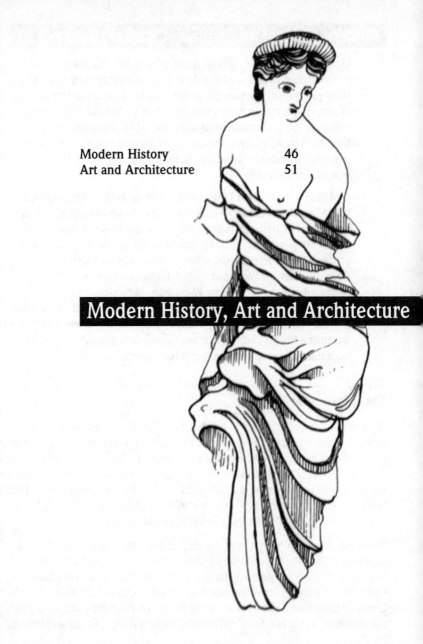

Modern History, Art and Architecture

Modern Greece: An Outline of Recent History

Unless you're one of those dullards who unplug themselves from their earphones and novels only to take photographs of donkeys, then you'll want to meet the Greeks. Although the massive influx of foreign visitors in recent years has had an inevitable numbing effect on the traditional hospitality offered to strangers, you will find that almost everyone you meet is friendly and gracious, and the older islanders—especially in the small villages—full of wonderful stories.

And rare indeed is the Greek who avoids talking about politics. It was Aristotle, after all, who declared man to be a political animal and if Greeks today have any link with their Classical past it is in their enthusiasm for all things political. An enthusiasm especially evident during an election, when all means of transport to the Greek islands are swamped with Athenians returning to their native villages to vote. Some knowledge of modern history is essential in understanding current Greek views and attitudes, and for that reason the following outline is included. Ancient and Byzantine history, which touches Greece less closely today, is dealt with under Athens and the individual islands.

The Spirit of Independence

From ancient times to the end of the Byzantine Empire, Greek people lived not only within the boundaries of modern-day Greece but throughout Asia Minor, in particular that part of Asia Minor now governed by Turkey. Constantinople was their capital, and although founded as a new Rome by Constantine, it was Greek. Not even during the 400-year Turkish occupation did these people and their brethren in Europe stop considering themselves Greeks—and the Turks, for the most part, were content to let them be Greek as long as they paid their taxes.

The revolutionary spirit that swept through Europe at the end of the 18th and beginning of the 19th centuries did not fail to catch hold in Greece, by now more than weary of the lethargic inactivity and sporadic cruelties of the Ottomans. The Greek War of Independence was begun in the Peloponnese in 1821, and it continued for more than six years in a series of bloody atrocities and political intrigues and divisions. In the end the Great Powers, namely Britain, Russia and France, came to assist the Greek cause, especially in the decisive battle of Navarino (20 October 1827) which in effect gave the newly formed Greek government the Peloponnese and the peninsula up to a line between the cities of Arta and Volos. Count John Capodistria of Corfu, ex-secretary to the Tsar of Russia, became the first President of Greece. While a king was sought for the new state, Capodistria followed an independent policy which succeeded in offending the pro-British and pro-French factions in Greece—and also the powerful Mavromikhalis family who assassinated him in 1831. Before the subsequent anarchy spread too far, the Great Powers appointed Otho, son of King Ludwig I of Bavaria, as King of the Greeks.

The Great Idea

Under Otho began what was called The Great Idea of uniting all the lands of the Greek peoples with the motherland, although Athens lacked the muscle to do anything about it at the time. Otho was peaceably ousted in 1862 and the Greeks elected William George, son of the King of Denmark, as 'King of the Hellenes'. By this they meant all the Greek people, and not merely those within the borders of Greece. The National Assembly drew up a constitution in 1864 which made the nation officially a democracy under a king, a system that began to work practically under Prime Minister Kharilaos Trikoupis in 1875. With the long reign of George I, Greece began to develop with an economy based on sea trade. The Great Idea had to wait for an opportune moment to ripen into reality.

In 1910 the great statesman from Crete, Eleftherios Venizelos, became Prime Minister of Greece for the first time. Under his direction the opportune moment came in the form of the two Balkan Wars of 1912–13, as a result of which Crete, Samos, Macedonia and southern Epirus were annexed to Greece. In the meantime King George was assassinated by a madman, and Constantine I ascended to the throne of Greece. Constantine had married the sister of Kaiser Wilhelm and had a close relationship with Germany, and when the First World War broke out, so did a dispute as to whose side Greece was on. Venizelos supported the Allies and Constantine the Central Powers, although he officially remained neutral until the Allies forced him to mobilize the Greek army. Meanwhile, in the north of Greece, Venizelos had set up his own government with volunteers in support of the Allied cause.

After the war to end all wars The Great Idea still smouldered, and Venizelos made the blunder of his career by sending Greek forces to occupy Smyrna (present-day Izmir) and advance on Ankara, the new Turkish capital. It was a disaster. The Turks, under Mustapha Kemal (later Ataturk) had grown far more formidable after their defeat in the Balkan War than the Greeks had imagined. In August 1922 the Greek army was completely routed at Smyrna, and many Greek residents who could not escape were slaughtered. Constantine immediately abdicated in favour of his son George II, and died soon afterwards. The government fell and Colonel Plastiras with his officers took over, ignobly executing the ministers of the previous government. Massive population exchanges were made between Greece and Turkey to destroy the rationale behind Greek expansionist claims, and the Greeks were confronted with the difficulties of a million Anatolian refugees.

In 1929 a republic was proclaimed which lasted for ten shaky years, during which the Greek communist party, or KKE, was formed and gained strength. After the brief Panglos dictatorship, the Greeks elected Venizelos back as President. He set the present borders of Greece (except for the Dodecanese Islands, which belonged to Italy until 1945). During his term of office there was also an unsuccessful uprising by the Greek Cypriots, four-fifths of the population of what was then a British Crown Colony, who desired union with Greece.

World War–Civil War

The republic, beset with economic difficulties, collapsed in 1935, and King George II returned to Greece, with General Metaxas as his Prime Minister. Metaxas took dictatorial control under the regime of 4 August, which crushed the trade unions and all leftist activities, exiling the leaders. Having prepared the Greek army long in advance for the coming war, Metaxas died in 1941 after his historic 'No!' to Mussolini. In 1940, with Italian troops on the Albanian border, Greece was the first Allied country voluntarily to join Britain against the Axis. The Greek army stopped the Italians and then pushed them back into Albania.

But by May 1941 all of Greece was in the hands of the Nazis, and George II was in exile in Egypt. The miseries of Occupation were compounded by political strife, fired by the uncertain constitutionality of a monarch who had been acting for so many years without parliamentary support. The Communist-organized EAM, the National Liberation Front, attacked all the competing resistance groups so rigorously that they came to support the monarchy as a lesser evil than the Communists. These Monarchists were supported in turn by the British. Nothing could be done, however, to prevent Civil War from breaking out three months after the liberation of Greece. The army of the EAM almost took Athens before the King finally agreed not to return to Greece without a plebiscite.

After the World War and the Civil War the country was in a shambles, economically and politically. Americans began to supersede the British in Greek affairs, and acted as observers in the elections of March 1946. A few months later the King was officially welcomed back to Greece, although he died a year later to be succeeded by his brother Paul.

Recovery and the Issue of Cyprus

Recovery was very slow, despite American assistance. Stalin also became very interested in the strategic location of Greece. In a roundabout way this caused the second Civil War in 1947 between the Communists and the government. The Americans became deeply involved defending the recent Truman Doctrine (on containing Communism, especially in Greece) and government forces finally won in October 1949, allowing the country to return to the problems of reconstruction.

With the Korean War in 1951 Greece and Turkey became full members of NATO, although the Cyprus issue again divided the two countries. In 1954, the Greek Cypriots, led by Archbishop Makarios, clamoured and rioted for union with Greece. Either for military reasons (so believe the Greeks) or to prevent a new conflict between Greece and Turkey, the Americans and British were hardly sympathetic to Cyprus' claims. Meanwhile Prime Minister Papagos died, and Konstantinos Karamanlis replaced him, staying in office for eight years. The stability and prosperity begun under Papagos increased, and agriculture and tourism began to replace Greece's traditional reliance on the sea. The opposition to Karamanlis criticized him for his pro-Western policy, basically because of the Cyprus bugbear, which grew worse all the time. Because of the island's one-fifth Turkish population and its strategic location, the Turks would not agree on union for Cyprus—the independence or partitioning of the island was as far as they would go. Finally in 1960, after much discussion on all sides, Cyprus became an independent republic and elected Makarios its first President. The British and Americans were considered to be good friends again.

Then once more the economy began to plague the government. The royal family became unpopular, there were strikes, and in 1963 came the assassination of Deputy Lambrakis in Thessaloniki (see the film *Z*) for which police officers were tried and convicted. Anti-Greek government feelings rose in London, just when the King and Queen were about to visit. Karamanlis advised them not to go, and their insistence sparked off his resignation. George Papandreou of the opposition was eventually elected Prime Minister. King Paul died and Constantine II became King of Greece.

In 1964 violence broke out in Cyprus again, owing to the disproportional representation in government of the Turkish minority. A quarrel with the King led to Papandreou's resignation resulting in much bitterness. The party system deteriorated and on 21 April 1967 a group of colonels established a military dictatorship. George Papandreou and his son Andreas were imprisoned, the latter charged with treason. Col. George Papadopoulos became dictator, imprisoning thousands without trial. In 1967 another grave incident occurred in Cyprus, almost leading to war. King Constantine II fled to Rome.

Moral Cleansing

The proclaimed aim of the colonels' junta was a moral cleansing of 'Christian Greece'. Human rights were suppressed, and the secret police tortured dissidents—or their children. Yet the British and American governments tolerated the regime, the latter very actively because of NATO. The internal situation went from bad to worse, and in 1973 students of the Polytechnic school in Athens struck. Tanks were brought in and many were killed. After this incident popular feeling rose to such a pitch that Papadopoulos was arrested, only to be replaced by his arrester, the head of the military police and an even worse dictator, Ioannides. The nation was in turmoil. Attempting to save his position by resorting to The Great Idea, Ioannides tried to launch a coup in Cyprus by assassinating Makarios, intending to replace him with a president who would declare the long-desired union of Cyprus with Greece. It was a fiasco. Makarios fled, and the Turkish army invaded Cyprus. The dictatorship resigned and Karamanlis returned to Athens from Paris where he had been living in exile. He immediately formed a new government, released the political prisoners and legalized the Communist party. He then turned his attention to Cyprus, where Turkish forces had occupied 40% of the island. But the Greek army was not strong enough to take on the Turks, nor did the position taken by the British and the American governments help.

Today's Republic

On 17 November 1974 an election was held, which Karamanlis easily won. The monarchy did less well and Greece became the republic it is today. In 1977 Archbishop Makarios died leaving the Cyprus issue unresolved in the minds of the Greeks, although the Turks seem to consider it well nigh settled. This remains one of the major debating points in Greek politics. The desire for social reform and an independent foreign policy were to be the ticket to Andreas Papandreou's Socialist victories in the 1980s. His party, PASOK, promised withdrawal from NATO and the removal of US air bases, along with many other far-reaching reforms. In practice, the new government found these impossible to implement, and the arrogant Papandreou succeeded in alienating nearly all of Greece's allies while overseeing a remarkable economic boom, thanks to the growth of tourism and EC loan money. In the end, scandals and corruption brought PASOK down; Papandreou's open affair with a much younger woman—Dimitri Liani, now his wife—and the Bank of Crete corruption scandal didn't go down well in an essentially conservative country. This led to PASOK losing power in 1990.

Mitsotakis and the New Democracy (ND) conservatives took a slim majority in the elections to grapple with Greece's economic problems. ND immediately launched a wave of austerity measures which proved even more unpopular than Papandreou—a crackdown on tax evasion, which is rife in Greece; a wage freeze for civil servants; privatisation of most state-run companies, including Olympic Airways; and steep increases in charges for public services. This sparked off a wave of strikes in 1991 and 1992. By late 1992 Mitsotakis was also involved in political scandals, and in 1993 a splinter party formed, Political Spring, led by Antonis Samaras. The principal effect of this was to split the votes and thereby topple ND when a general election was held in October 1993.

PASOK, led again by the ageing Andreas Papandreou, won the election, and proceeded to build a political dynasty that would make Bill Clinton jealous; he appointed his young wife as chief of staff, made his son the deputy foreign minister, and even made his own doctor the minister of health. 75-year-old Papandreou's own health is poor, and most Greeks doubt his ability to administer the medicine Greece needs. The big issues on the agenda for the next year or so are the continuing economic problems, the rising foreign debt, the influx of Albanian refugees, and the Macedonian question, on which Greece seems prepared to defy all of her allies, even at the risk of igniting an all-out Balkan war.

A Brief Outline of Greek Art and Architecture

Neolithic to 3000 BC

The oldest known settlements on the Greek islands date back to approximately 6000 BC—Knossos, Phaistos and the cave settlements of **Crete**, obsidian-exporting Phylokope on **Milos**, sophisticated Paleochoe on **Limnos** and Ag. Irene on **Kea**. Artistic finds are typical of the era elsewhere—dark burnished pottery, decorated with spirals and wavy lines and statuettes of the fertility goddess in stone or terra cotta.

Bronze Age: Cycladic and Minoan styles (3000–1100 BC)

Contacts with Anatolia and the Near East brought Crete and the Cyclades to the cutting edge of not only Greek, but European civilization. Around 2600 BC Cycladic dead were buried with extraordinary white marble figurines, or idols that border on the modern abstract (in the museums in **Naxos** and **Athens**). In the same period the first Minoans in Crete were demonstrating an uncanny artistic talent in their polychrome pottery—Kamares ware—and their stone vases (carved to resemble ceramic) and gold jewellery. They buried their dead in round *tholos* tombs up to 18 m in diameter. Hieroglyphs, learned from the Egyptians, were used to keep track of the magazines of oil, wine and grain stored in huge *pithoi* which characterize Minoan palaces and villas.

By the Middle Minoan period (2000–1700 BC) Crete ruled the Aegean with its mighty fleet. The Minoan priest-kings were secure enough from external and internal threats to build themselves unfortified palaces and cities, inevitably centred around a large rectangular courtyard. They installed a system of canals and drains which suggests that the Romans were hardly the first to take regular baths. Hieroglyphic writing was replaced by the still undeciphered script Linear A. Cretan civilization reached its apogee in the Late Minoan period (1700–1450 BC), when the Minoans had colonies across the Aegean and their elegant ambassadors figured in the tomb paintings of the Pharaohs; their own palaces at **Knossos, Phaistos, Zakros, Mallia** and at their outpost of Akrotiri on the island of **Santorini** were adorned with elegant frescoes of flowers, animals, human figures and bull dancers and other treasures now in the archaeology museums of **Herakleon** and **Athens**.

Built mostly of wood and unbaked brick, the Minoan palaces collapsed like card castles in a great natural disaster when the volcanic island of Santorini exploded *c.* 1450 BC. The Achaeans of Mycenae rushed in to fill the vacuum of power and trade in the Aegean, taking over the Minoan colonies; their influence extended to the language of Linear B, which has been deciphered as a form of early Greek. The Achaeans adopted the Minoans' artistic techniques, especially in goldwork and ceramics. Little of this ever reached the islands, although many have vestiges of the Achaeans' stone walls, known as *cyclopean* after their gigantic blocks. As impressive as they are, they failed to keep out the northern invaders known as the Dorians, who destroyed Aegean unity and ushered in one of history's perennial Dark Ages.

Geometric (1000–700 BC) and Archaic (700–500 BC)

The break-up of the Minoan and Mycenaean world saw a return to agriculture and the development of the *polis* or city-state. In art the Geometric period refers to the simple, abstract decoration of the pottery; traces of Geometric temples of brick and wood are much rarer. The temple of Apollo at **Dreros** on Crete and the first Temple of Hera on **Samos** were built around the 8th century, although both pale before the discovery in 1981 of the huge sanctuary at **Lefkandi** on Evia, believed to date from *c.* 900 BC. The most complete Geometric town discovered so far is Zagora on **Andros**.

The Archaic Period is marked by the change to stone, especially limestone, for the building of temples and a return to representational art in decoration. The first known stone temple—and a prototype of the Classical temple with its columns, pediments and metopes—was **Corfu**'s stout-columned Doric Temple of Artemis (580 BC), its pediment decorated with a formidable 10-ft Medusa (now in Corfu's museum). The beautiful Doric Temple of Aphaia on **Aegina** was begun in the same period and decorated with a magnificent 6th-century pediment sculpted with scenes from the Trojan war (now in Munich). The excavations at Emborio, on **Chios**, are among the best extant records we have of an Archaic town; the 6th-century Efplinion tunnel at Pythagorio, **Samos** was the engineering feat of the age.

This era also saw the beginning of life size—and larger—figure sculpture, inspired by the Egyptians: poses are stiff, formal, and rigid, one foot carefully placed before the other. The favourite masculine figure was the *kouros*, or young man, originally one of the dancers at fertility ritual (see the marble quarries of **Naxos** and the *Kriophoros* of **Thassos**); the favourite feminine figure was the *kore*, or maiden, dressed in graceful drapery, representing Persephone and the return of spring. The Archaeology Museum in **Athens** has the best examples of both. The 7th century also saw the development of regional schools of pottery, influenced by the black-figured techniques of Corinth: **Rhodes** and the Cycladic islands produced some of the best.

Classic (500–380 BC)

As Athens became the dominant power in the Aegean, it attracted much of the artistic talent of the Greek world and concentrated its most refined skills on its showpiece Acropolis, culminating with the extraordinary mathematical precision and perfect proportions of the Parthenon, the greatest of all Doric temples, yet built without a single straight line in the entire building. Nothing on the islands approaches it, although there are a few classical-era sites to visit: **Limen** on Thassos and **Eretria** on Evia, **Lindos, Kamiros** and **Ialysos** on Rhodes.

Hellenistic (380–30 BC)

This era brought new stylistic influences from the eastern lands, conquered and hellenized by Alexander the Great and his lieutenants. Compared to the cool, aloof perfection of the Classical era, Hellenistic sculpture is characterized by a more emotional, Mannerist approach, of windswept drapery, violence, and passion. Much of what remains of **Samothrace**'s Sanctuary of the Great Gods, and the Louvre's dramatic *Victory of Samothrace* are from the Hellenistic period. Ancient Rhodes was at the height of its powers, and produced its long-gone Colossus, as well as the writhing *Laocoon* (now in the Vatican museum) and Aphrodite statues in the **Rhodes** museum. Houses became decidedly more plush, many decorated with mosaics and frescoes as in the commercial town of **Delos** and in the suburbs of **Kos**.

Roman (30 BC–AD 529)

The Pax Romana ended the rivalries between the Greek city-states and pretty much ended the source of their artistic inspiration, although sculptors, architects, and other talents found a ready market for their skills in Rome, cranking out copies of Classic and Hellenistic masterpieces. The Romans themselves built little in Greece: the stoa and theatre of Heroditus Atticus (160 AD) were the last large monuments erected in ancient Athens. On the islands, the largest site is **Gortyna**, the Roman capital of Crete.

Byzantine (527–1460)

The art and architecture of the Byzantine Empire began to show its stylistic distinction under the reign of Justinian (527–565), and the immediate post-Justinian period saw a first golden age in the splendour of Ag. Sofia in Istanbul and the churches of Ravenna, Italy. On the islands you'll find only the remains of simple three-naved basilicas—with two important exceptions: the 6th-century Ekatontapyliani of **Paros** and 7th-century Ag. Titos at **Gortyna**, Crete.

After the austere anti-art puritanism of the Iconoclasm (726–843) the Macedonian style (named after the Macedonian emperors) slowly infiltrated the Greek provinces. The old Roman basilica plan was jettisoned in favour of what became the classic Byzantine style: a central Greek-cross plan crowned by a dome, elongated in front by a vestibule (narthex) and outer porch (exonarthex) and in the back by a choir and three apses. **Dafni** just outside Athens and Nea Moni on **Chios** with its massive cupola, are superb examples; both are decorated with extraordinary mosaics from the second golden age of Byzantine art, under the dynasty of the Comnenes (12th–14th centuries). As in Italy, this period marked a renewed interest in antique models: the stiff, elongated hieratic figures with staring eyes have more naturalistic proportions in graceful, rhythmic compositions; good examples are at **Dafni**. The age of the Comnenes also produced some fine painting: the 12th-century frescoes and manuscripts at the Monastery of St John on **Patmos**; the beautifully-frescoed early 13th-century Kera Panayia at **Kritsa**, near Ag. Nikolaos on Crete. Crete's occupation by Venice after 1204 marked the beginning of an artistic cross-fertilization that developed into the highly-esteemed Cretan school of icon painting, most conveniently seen in the Byzantine museums in Ag. Katerina in **Herakleon** and in **Athens**.

What never changed was the intent of Byzantine art, which is worth a small digression because in the 14th century Western sacred art went off in an entirely different direction—so much so that everything before is disparagingly labelled 'primitive' in most art books. One of the most obvious differences is the strict iconography in Byzantine painting: if you know the code you can instantly identify each saint by the cut of beard or his or her attribute. Their appeal to the viewer, even in the 11th century when the figures were given more naturalistic proportions, is equally purely symbolic; a Byzantine Christ on the Cross, the Virgin *Panayia*, the 'all-holy', angels, saints and martyrs never make a play for the heartstrings, but reside on a purely spiritual and intellectual plane. As Patrick Leigh Fermor wrote: 'Post-primitive religious painting in the West is based on horror, physical charm, infant-worship and easy weeping.' Icons and Byzantine frescoes never ask the viewer to relive vicariously the passion of Christ or coo over Baby Jesus; Byzantine angels never lift their draperies to reveal a little leg; the remote, wide-eyed Panayia has none of the luscious charms of the Madonna. They never stray from their remote otherworldliness.

And yet, in the last gasp of Byzantine art under the Paleologos emperors (14th–early 15th centuries), humanist and naturalistic influences combined to produce the Byzantine equivalent of the Late Gothic/early Renaissance painting in Italy, in Mistras in the Peloponnese. It is the great might-have-been of Byzantine art: after the Turkish conquest the best painters took refuge on Mount Athos, or on the islands ruled by Venice, but none of their work radiates the same charm or confidence in the temporal world.

Turkish Occupation to the Present

The Turks left few important monuments in Greece, and much of what they did build was wrecked by the Greeks after independence. **Rhodes** town has the best surviving mosques, hammams, houses and public buildings, not only because the Turks loved it well, but because it only became Greek in 1945. **Crete** and **Corfu** have a number of fine Venetian relics: impressive fortifications and gates, fountains, public buildings and town houses. Elsewhere, islands with their own fleets, especially **Hydra**, **Spetses** and **Symi** have impressive captain's mansions, while other islands continued traditional architectural styles: the whitewashed asymmetry of the Cyclades, the patterned sgraffito in the mastic villages of Chios, the Macedonian wooden upper floors and balconies of the northernmost islands.

In the 19th century, public buildings in both Athens and **Syros** (briefly Greece's chief port) are fairly bland neo-Classical works; a host of neo-Byzantine churches went up, while many older ones were unfortunately tarted up with tired bastard painting, Byzantine in iconography but most of it no better than the contents of a third rate provincial museum in Italy.

On the whole, the less said about 20th century architecture on the islands the better: the Fascist architecture left by the Italians on the Dodecanese islands has a sense of style, which is more than can be said of the cheap concrete slabs that have gone up elsewhere. Prosperity in the 1980s has brought an increased interest in local architecture and historic preservation: following the lead of the National Tourist Organization's traditional settlement programme, private individuals have begun to restore old monasteries, abandoned villages, and captains' mansions, while many of the newest resort developments are less brash and more in harmony with local styles. One individual who won't be restoring any of his Palaces is ex-King Constantine of Greece, whose properties were expropriated by the Papandraeus Government in 1994.

Topics

The signs at Athens Airport proclaim: Macedonia is Greek. If that doesn't sink in, then the slogans on the new phonecards drive the message home: Macedonia is One and Only and it is Greek. And don't think you can escape hearing about the issue by flying off to the distant islands; the Greeks are obsessed with the subject, and it's worth knowing some historical background in case you become embroiled in a discussion about it.

The Greek government, and the nation, emphatically denies recognition of the independent Republic of Macedonia in the former Yugoslavia. Ever since the province bordering Greek Macedonia declared itself independent and adopted the M-word in April 1993, nationalistic fervour has broken out and the Greeks are outraged, wearing lapel pins featuring the symbol of Alexander the Great, Macedonia's most famous son.

Ironically Greece, host nation of the EC in 1994, is pitting itself against EC moves to recognize the former Yugoslav state. Campaigners argue that Macedonia has been Greek for 3,000 years (some claim 4,000 years), and thus has a copyright on the name. They fear borders will be re-drawn, there is even threat of invasion, and say Ancient Macedonia was a Hellenistic civilisation, not a Slavic one, as the Slavs didn't settle on the Balkan peninsula until the 6th century AD.

Macedon was a backwoods kingdom on the fringes of Greek civilization until the advent of Philip II (reigned 359–336 BC), who, aided by the discovery of gold and his own unconventional military tactics, created the most effective army in Greece. As the Greek states squabbled among themselves, he annexed Thessaly (352 BC), and in 338 BC gobbled up the rest of Greece by crushing the last-minute anti-Macedonian coalition of Athens and Thebes. Philip forced the city-states into a pan-Hellenic league that took orders from him. The first was to raise a massive army against the Persians. Philip was assassinated, leaving the vast army to his son Alexander, who had been carefully groomed to think like a true Greek by the greatest teacher of the day—Aristotle.

Alexander had inherited all of his father's military genes, and then some. After a quick razing of Thebes to keep the quarrelsome Greeks in their place, he took his pan-Hellenic army to Persia and began his inexorable conquest that stretched to India before his army staged a sit-down strike and refused to march another step. Although much of his great empire died with him or was divided up into chunks by his generals (his Ptolemies in Egypt, the Seleucids of Syria), his greatest achievment in the eyes of the Greeks was the hellenisation (read civilisation) of his conquests. Greek became the lingua franca and the gods of Olympus usurped the temples of their barbaric brethren. Yet during his lifetime, Alexander was looked down on by the Greeks as little more than a barbarian himself.

From 215–146 BC Rome meddled increasingly in Greek affairs, at first participating in the Macedonian Wars between Philip V of Macedon and the rival Aetolian and Achaian federations. Philip was forced into an alliance with Rome in 200 BC and the Macedon kingdom was destroyed in 168 BC to become the Roman province of Macedonia; under the later Ottoman empire the population of Macedonia, a region with hazily-defined borders, was such a mixture of Greeks, Albanians, Serbs, Bulgarians and Romanians that it gave rise to the French word for salad (*macédoine*).

As the Ottoman Empire died its slow death in the early 1990s, Macedonia became a hotbed of rival nationalistic groups. When the two Balkan wars erupted in 1912 Greece gained southern Macedonia, Salonika and Kavala, just beating the Bulgarians in the rush for territory. Disagreements over the borders have rankled ever since; in the murky Balkan fruit salad names count for a lot.

Fiercely proud and defensive after centuries of domination, the Greeks believe it is an outrage for the name of Macedonia to be adopted by the former Yugoslav state. To them the golden age of their cultural history has been usurped and acceptance of any EC recognition is unlikely.

Natural History

For years Greek environmentalists have pushed for legislation to protect rare species of wildlife in the Aegean and Ionian Seas. National parks, wildlife sanctuaries and hunting laws are well regulated on the mainland, but it is the fragile ecosystems of the dying seas that cry out most desperately for protection. In the early 1980s, efforts to save the Mediterranean green loggerhead turtle centred on Zakynthos; information kiosks sprouted on the island, representing not only a conscious effort to protect marine life, but also the first public information outlets directly in conflict with the mighty gods of tourism. Because the turtles lay their eggs on the sandy beaches, sometimes immediately in front of resort hotels, the noise, lights, and innocent trampling of buried turtle eggs was destroying a turtle population already struggling against a hundred natural predators. Controls and schedules were imposed on the use of beaches by tourists, infuriating local proprietors who saw their incomes threatened, while to environmentalists, who considered tourists little better than 'terrorists' the regulations hardly went far enough. Gradually both sides have moderated their stance to reach a compromise: tourists must respect the turtles, an attitude that has proved profitable in drawing eco-tourists.

The biggest hurdle faced by Greek environmentalists is the lack of local support. Business people fear that even the slightest restrictions on tourist activity will make tourists and their money stay away. The facts prove the contrary. Island councils, restaurants, hotels and tour boat operators are gradually becoming aware that people long to go to places where the environment is healthy and clean. They are happy to see wildlife in its natural habitat, even if only a glimpse. Tourists tend to return to places with natural beauty, enticed by harmony with nature, and locals are slowly beginning to realize that Greece fits the bill.

As for creatures unfortunately *not* on the endangered list, the wily mosquito tops the list for pure incivility. Most shops stock the usual defences: lotions, sprays and insect coils; or pick up one of those inexpensive electric mosquito repellents that fit right in the wall plug and don't stink as badly as the smouldering coils. The most effective repellents contain high proportions of Deet; Autan and Jungle Formula (on sale in the UK, sometimes from airport chemists) do the job. Jungle Formula contains more Deet and tends to be more effective.

Public insect enemy Number Two is the wasp, either taking bites out of that honey baklava you've just ordered, or spoiling your picnic on the beach (a special hazard on the lush Ionian islands). Dangers lurk in the sea as well: harmless pale brown jellyfish (*médusas*) may drift in anywhere depending on winds and currents, but the oval transparent model (*tsouitres*) are stinging devils that can leave scars on tender parts of your anatomy if you brush against them. Pincushiony black sea urchins live on the rocks of rocky beaches, and must be avoided. The spines may break and embed themselves, deeper still if you try to force them out; the Greeks recommend olive oil and a lot of patience to get the spine to slip out. As first aid, they suggest peeing on them to take away the sting (if you're a woman, summon a friend). They hurt like hell, so on rocky beaches it makes sense to wear sandals or plastic shoes in the water if you're likely to be putting your feet down on the rocks.

Much less common are Greece's shy scorpions, who hide out in between the rocks in rural areas; unless you're especially sensitive, their sting is no more nor less painful than a bee's. Always avoid the back legs of mules, unless you've been properly introduced. The really lethal creatures are rare: the small, grey-brown viper that lives in the nooks and crannies of stone walls, where it is well camouflaged, only comes out occasionally to sun itself. Although it is seldom seen (it prefers abandoned villages and quiet archaeological sites), the Greeks are terri-fied of it; the mere word *fithi* (snake) will turn the most stout-hearted villager to jelly. Mountain sheepdogs are a more immediate danger in outer rural areas; by stooping as if to pick up a stone to throw, you might keep a dog at bay.

Sharks seldom prowl near the coastal regions of Greece. Blood attracts them, so if you are wounded, swim for shore without delay. Divers should ask their Greek confrères about other dangerous fish in the area, such as the weaver, an unlikely delicacy whose razor-sharp fins can kill.

On *Kefi* and Dancing

In the homogenized European Community of the 1990s, only the Spaniards and Greeks still dance to their own music with any kind of spontaneity, and it's no coincidence that both have untranslatable words to describe the 'spirit' or 'mood' that separates going through the steps and true dancing. In Spain, the word is *duende*, which, with the hard driving rhythms of flamenco, has an ecstatic quality; in Greek, the word is *kefi*, which comes closer to 'soul'. For a Greek to give his all, he must have *kefi*; to dance without it could be considered dishonest. The smart young men in black trousers and red sashes who dance for you at dinner probably don't have it; two craggy old fishermen, in a smoky café in Crete, who crank up an old gramophone and dance for their own pleasure, do. You can feel the *kefi* at Easter when the village elders join hands and dance an elegant *kalamatiano*, or when a group of children celebrate the local saint's day in North Karpathos. Any sensitive person can't help but be moved by the atmosphere, especially in contrast with the stark, technically perfect stage performances of the dance troupes under the Acropolis or in the old fort of Corfu. If the *kefi* moves you to leap up and dance, your Greek friends will see you in a new light, your bond with Greece established, and you may find it just that bit harder to book your ticket home.

Nearly every island has its own dance, some of which are extremely difficult. Then there are the dances everyone knows, from the elementary 'one two three kick kick', or *Sta Tria*, footed in a circle with hands on shoulders. The circle is never complete, however: even in this simple dance a man or woman will lead, handkerchief in hand, setting the pace and supplying the special effects with leaps, foot slaps, kicks, little skips or whatever he or she likes. Cretans are among the most energetic leaders—some are almost contortionists.

Sta Tria often begins slowly and picks up to a furious pace towards the end. The *sýrto*, on the other hand, retains its slow graceful pace throughout. It has only six easy steps which are repeated until the end, but watch the leader for variations. This is considered the oldest Greek dance of all, dating back to Hellenistic, if not Homeric times. The *kalamatíanos*, a 12-step dance, takes some practice. If a Greek invites you to dance the *bállos*, the most common couple's dance, follow your partner's lead and hope for the best. While there are certain set steps to the *tsiftetéli*, or belly dance, it has become a free-spirited dance for the loose limbed and requires plenty of nerve (or wine) to pull off successfully.

The *zembekiko* is normally but not exclusively performed by men, a serious, deliberate solo dance with outstretched arms, evoking the swooping flight of the eagle; a companion will go down on one knee to encourage the dancer and clap out the rhythm. The *hasápiko*, better known as the Zorba dance, and traditionally performed by two men, will require some practice but is well worth learning—like Alan Bates who finally began to fathom *kefi* from Anthony Quinn at the end of the film *Zorba the Greek*. Plenty of practice and energy are the rules for joining in most Cretan dances, where the music demands furious, machine-gun fire steps and hops that go on until your adrenalin has pumped its last. But toss back another *raki*, and before you know it you'll be up dancing another *pentozal* or *podokto*.

You can get off on the right foot with *Greek Dances* by Ted Petrides (published by Lycabettus Press in Athens), supplemented by some private coaching from the Greeks—or their children, who usually have more patience.

Orthodoxy

With the exception of a handful of Catholics in the Cyclades, nearly all Greeks belong to the Orthodox, or Eastern church; indeed, being Orthodox and speaking Greek are the two most important criteria in defining a Greek, whether born in Athens, Alexandria or Australia. Orthodoxy is so fundamental that even the greatest sceptics can hardly conceive of marrying outside the church, or neglecting to have their children baptized.

One reason for this deep national feeling is that unlike everything else in Greece, Orthodoxy has scarcely changed since the founding of the church by Constantine in the 4th century. As Constantinople took the place of Rome as the political and religious capital, the Greeks believe their church to be the only true successor to the original church of Rome. Therefore, a true Greek is called a *Romiós* or Roman, and the Greek language of today is called *Romaíka*. It is considered perfect and eternal and beyond all worldly change; if it weren't, its adherents could not expect to be saved. Hence, the Greeks have been spared the changes that have rocked the West, from Vatican II to discussions over women in the clergy to political questions of abortion, birth control and so on—matters on which Orthodoxy has always remained aloof. Much emphasis is put on ceremony and ritual, the spiritual and aesthetic, with very little appeal to the emotions.

This explains the violence of Iconoclasm, the one movement to change the rules. Back in the early 8th century Byzantine Emperor Leo III the Isaurian, shamed by what his Moslem neighbours labelled idolatry, deemed the images of divine beings to be sacriligious. Iconoclasm began the rift with Rome, that worsened in 800 when the Pope crowned Charlemagne as emperor, usurping the position of the Emperor of Constantinople. Further divisions arose over the celibacy of the clergy (Orthodox may marry before they are ordained) and the use of the phrase 'and the son' in the Holy Creed, the issue which caused the final, fatal schism in 1054 when the Pope's representative Cardinal Humbert excommunicated the Patriarch of Constantinople.

After the fall of the Byzantine Empire (that 'thousand-year-long mass for the dead' as one recent Greek writer put it), the Turks not only tolerated the Orthodox church, but they had the political astuteness to impart considerable powers to the patriarch. The church was thus able to preserve many Greek traditions and Greek education through the dark age of Ottoman rule; on the other hand it often abused this power against its own flock, especially locally. According to an old saying, priests, headmen and Turks were the three curses of Greece and the poor priests (who in truth are usually quite amiable fellows) have not yet exonerated themselves from the list they now share with the king and the cuckold.

The extraordinary quantity of churches and chapels on some islands has little to do with the priests, however. Nearly all were built by families or individuals, especially by sailors, seeking the protection of a patron saint. Some were built to keep a promise, others in simple thanksgiving. Architecturally they come in an endless variety of styles depending on the region, period and terrain, as well as the wealth and whim of the builder. All but the tiniest have an *iconostasis*, or altar screen, made of wood or stone to separate the *heiron* or sanctuary, where only the ordained are allowed, from the rest of the church. Most of the chapels are now locked up; some light-fingered tourists have decided that icons make lovely souvenirs; if you track down the caretaker, do dress discreetly (no shorts!) and leave a few drachmas for upkeep.

Almost all these chapels have only one service a year, on the name day of the patron saint (name days are celebrated in Greece more widely than birthdays: 'Many years!' *(Chrónia pollá!)* is the proper way to greet someone on their name day). This annual celebration is called a *yiortí* or more frequently *paniyiri*, and is the cause for feasts and dancing before or after the church service. If feasible, *paniyiria* take place directly in the churchyard, if not, in neighbouring wooded areas or in tavernas. The food can be superb but is more often basic and plentiful; for a set price you receive more than your share and a doggy bag full, generally of goat. *Paniyiria* (festivals) are also the best places to hear traditional island music and learn the dances, and it's sad that they're only a fond memory in most major tourist centres (although alive and well in less frequented areas). The Assumption of the Virgin, 15 August, is the largest *paniyiri* in Greece apart from Easter, the biggest holiday. The faithful sail to Tinos, the Lourdes of Greece, and to a dozen centres connected with Mary, making mid-August a very uncomfortable time to travel among the islands, especially the Cyclades. Not only are the ships packed to the brim, but the *meltemi* wind also blows with vigour, and Greek matrons, the most ardent pilgrims of all, are the worst of all sailors.

Orthodox weddings are another lovely if long-winded ritual. The bride and groom stand solemnly before the chanting priest, while family and friends in attendance seem to do everything but follow the proceedings. White crowns, bound together by a white ribbon, are placed on the heads of bride and groom, and the *koumbáros*, or best man, exchanges them back and forth. The newlyweds are then led around the altar three times, which spurs the guests into action as they bombard the happy couple with fertility-bringing rice and flower petals. After congratulating the bride and groom guests are given a small *boboniéra* of sugared almonds. This is followed by the marriage feast and dancing, which in the past could last up to five days. If you are in the vicinity of a village wedding you may be offered a sweet cake; you may even be invited to come along to the feasting as a special guest.

Baptisms are cause for similar celebration. The priest completely immerses the baby in the Holy Water three times (unlike Achilles, there are no vulnerable spots on modern Greeks) and almost always gives the little one the name of a grand-parent. For extra protection from the forces of evil, babies often wear a *filaktó*, or amulet, the omnipresent blue glass eye bead. If you visit a baby at home you may well be sprinkled first with Holy Water, and chances are there's a bit of beneficial garlic squeezed somewhere under the cradle. Compliments to the little one's parents should be kept to a minimum; the gods do get jealous.

Funerals in Greece, for reasons of climate, are carried out as soon as possible, and are announced by the tolling of the village church bells. The dead are buried for three to five years (longer if the family can pay) after which time the bones are exhumed and placed in the family box to make room for the next resident. *Aforismós*, or Orthodox excommunication, is believed to prevent the body decaying after death—the main source of Greek vampire stories. Memorials for the dead take place three, nine and forty days after death, and on the first anniversary. They are sometimes repeated annually. Sweet buns and sugared wheat and raisin *koúliva* are given out after the ceremony; children wouldn't miss them for the world.

The *Periptero* and the Plane Tree

In Greece you'll see it everywhere, the greatest of modern Greek inventions, the indispensable *periptero*. It is the best-equipped kiosk in the world, where people gather to chat, make local or international calls, or grab a few minutes' shade under the little projecting roof. The *periptero* is a substitute bar, selling everything from water to cigarettes to ice cold beer; an emergency pharmacy stocked with aspirin, mosquito killers, condoms and sticking plaster; a convenient newsagent for Greek and international publications, from *Ta Nea* to *Die Zeit*; a tourist shop offering travel guides, postcards and stamps; a toy shop for balloons, plastic swords and My Little Pony; a general store for shoelaces, batteries and rolls of film. In Athens they're at most traffic lights. On the islands they are a more common sight than a donkey. You'll wonder how you ever survived before *peripteros* and the treasures they contain.

The other great meeting centre of Greek life is the mighty plane tree, or *platanos*, for centuries the focal point of village life, where politics and philosophy have been argued since time immemorial. Since Hippocrates the Greeks have believed that plane shade is wholesome and beneficial (unlike the ennervating shadow cast by the fig) and one of the most extraordinary sights in the islands is 'Hippocrates' plane tree' on Kos in the Dodecanese, propped up on scaffolding and as protected as any national monument would be. In Greek the expression *herete mou ton platano* loosely translates as 'go tell it to the marines', presumably because the tree has heard all that nonsense before. For a Greek village the *platanos* represents that village's identity; the tree is a source of life, for it only grows near abundant fresh water; its deep roots a symbol of stability, continuity and protection—a huge majestic umbrella, even the rain cannot penetrate its sturdy leaves. Sit under its spreading branches and sip a coffee as the morning unfolds before you; the temptation to linger there for the day is irresistible.

Shirley Valentines

Know thyself

–inscription over the gate of the oracle at Delphi

There isn't an island without at least one Shirley Valentine, drawn years ago by something special, a holiday romance perhaps that turned into a love affair with a place rather than a person, an enjoyment of living in a country where eccentrics are welcomed rather than scorned. Shirley Valentines come in all shapes and sizes, male or female, young or old, cynical or innocent, birdwatchers or bartenders, pensioners from New York, English gym teachers and marine insurance agents, lost souls from Hamburg, Dutch advertising execs, an occasional black sheep or social misfit; all characters who have found their Atlantis, and can now only live as strange birds in foreign nests.

These people have become part of island daily life and, as far as many locals are concerned, add a missing ingredient. They know their island well, and are usually a good source of information, whether it be tracking down the friendliest watering hole, or blackmailing the builder who promised to turn up weeks ago. Björn from Stockholm has been there for years, married a local girl and can outswear the locals. Penny from Bath can drink the village boys under the table. She has her reasons for doing so; her heart is broken with regularity, and every day brings tears and laughter, but turning Ipanemian brown under the Greek sun, far from the monochrome office blocks, and watching the sun set at the most beautiful time of the day brings a serenity and happiness previously unknown.

'Greece' once remarked President Karamanlis, 'reminds me of an enormous madhouse'. True or not, whether the Shirley Valentines have a streak of madness in them, Greece has allowed them to invent for themselves a way of living their fantasies, of building a new personality that was just under the surface anyway.

When You've Gone

As the days shorten and the cafés close, the last forlorn tourists sit on the deserted waterfront, and the empty echoes of summer fade away. There's now a chill to the wind as the waiters collect up the tables and chairs, no longer needed for the rest of the year, and the island returns to normality. The discotheques, not long ago throbbing to Right Said Fred, close down; the bouzouki replaces the electric guitar, boogie gives way to the *zembekiko* and the overall tempo of life changes. The real Greece re-emerges, the islanders claim back their island. Plastic cafés are re-transformed into lively little *ouzeri*, and it is time to sit and reflect on the summer, count the precious drachmas and lick wounds. The evening stroll, or *volta*, returns with full intensity, and the greeting is *Kalo chimona*, or 'Have a good winter'. Wild seas reclaim the beaches; the last Coca Cola can is washed away as the pebbles are rinsed of suntan lotion. Even the swallows decamp, and head south to warmer climes. As the wind kicks up, bare-bones ferry schedules go haywire; fresh vegetables, meat and milk become scarce on many islands, and many a meal consists of beans or lentils, sardines and pasta.

Cold, wet and windy, the Greek winter takes hold of the summer paradise, and men huddle in the *cafenia* discussing politics and tourist conquests, playing cards and *tavli* (backgammon), watching blue movies. Gambling becomes a craze in the winter and fortunes made in the summer can be lost at the turn of a card. Women stay at home and do their needlework or watch soaps on TV. The sun's warmth is replaced by the warmth of the family, and grandma can now take repossession of her little room rented out on the black to backpackers. The only voices in the main street are those of the children wandering in a ragged line to the village school, clutching their schoolbags and midday snacks of bread and spam. The few hardy perennial foreign residents make a reappearance in the cafés, and the lingua franca once again returns to demotic Greek.

The summer spirit flickers briefly in winter's depths, and the gentle sun sometimes provides enough warmth to sit out by the still, sparkling blue sea, watching the caiques come in with their haul. Spring, the loveliest of all seasons in Greece, sees the trees blossom and the islands transformed into carpets of flowers, as Easter approaches. Even the most boisterous Greeks are subdued in the week preceding the Easter weekend, which erupts into a frenzy of dancing, rejoicing, eating and drinking, as fireworks light up the midnight sky. *Christos anesti*! is the greeting, 'Christ has risen!' and millions of candles are lit around the country.

Like magic any harsh memories of the previous summer are forgotten, vendettas are forgiven, and a rejuvenated population prepares itself for a new season, painting café chairs, mending shopfronts, whitewashing walls. There's a feeling of expectancy in the air as, first the swallows, then the tourists arrive, and the whole show winds up again.

Athens and Piraeus

Many travellers to the Greek islands eventually find themselves in Athens and Piraeus, but it's rarely love at first sight; Athens, with its ramshackle architecture and grubby, dusty exterior, wins no beauty prizes. Look closely, however, and you may be won over by this urban crazy quilt of villages—small oases of green parks hidden amidst the hustle and bustle; tiny family-run tavernas tucked away in the most unexpected places; the feverish pace of its nightlife and summer festivals devoted to wine and song; and best all, the Athenians themselves, whose friendliness belies the reputation of most inhabitants of capital cities.

An Historical Outline of Athens

Inhabited by pre-Hellenic tribes in the Neolithic Age (c. 3500 BC) Athens made its proper debut on the stage of history in the second millennium, when Ionians from Asia Minor invaded Attica and established several small city-states. Their main centre was Kekropia, named for the serpent god Kekrops (he later became connected with King Erechtheus, who was himself a snake from the waist down and is considered to be the original founder of Athens). The owl was sacred to Kekropia—as it was to the goddess Athena, and her worship and name gradually came to preside in the city.

In the 14th century BC Athens, as part of the Mycenaean empire of the Achaeans, invaded Crete, fought Thebes, and conquered Troy, but managed to escape the subsequent Dorian invasion which brought chaos into the Mycenaean world. Two hundred years later, however, it was Attica's turn to meet the uncouth Dorians, who brought with them Greece's first Dark Age. This endured until the 8th century BC, far too long for the sophisticated Ionians and Aeolians, who went back to their homelands in Asia Minor and settled many of the Aegean islands.

Sometime during the 8th century all the towns of Attica were peaceably united, an accomplishment attributed to the mythical King Theseus (1300 BC). Athens was then ruled by a king (the chief priest), a *polemarch* (or general), and an *archon* (or civil authority), positions that became annually elective by the 6th century. The conflict between the landed aristocracy and rising commercial classes gradually brought about the solution of democratic government, beginning under the reforms of Solon. Yet under every stone there lurked a would-be tyrant; Solon was still warm in the grave when Pisistratos, leader of the popular party, made himself boss (545 BC) and began the naval build-up that first made Athens a threat to the other independent city-states of Greece.

Pisistratos' son was followed by another reformer, Kleisthenes, who discarded Athens' ancient but unsatisfactory political classifications by dividing the population into ten tribes. Each selected by lot 50 members of the people's assembly, from which a further lot was drawn to select an archon, creating ten archons in all, one from each tribe. The head archon gave his name to the Athenian year.

Meanwhile, as Persian strength grew in the east, Ionian intellectuals and artists settled in Athens, bringing with them the roots of Attic tragedy. They encouraged Athens to aid the Ionians against the Persians, an unsuccessful adventure that landed the city in the soup when Darius, the King of Kings, turned to subdue Greece, and in particular Athens, which posed the only threat to the Persian fleet. In 490 BC Darius' vast army landed at Marathon only to be defeated by a much smaller Athenian force under Miltiades. Powerful Sparta and the other Greek states then recognized the eastern threat, but continued to leave 'national' defence primarily in the hands of the Athenians and their fleet, which grew ever mightier under Themistocles. However, it failed to keep the Persians from having another go at Greece, and in 480 BC the new king Xerxes showed up with the greatest fleet and army the ancient world had ever seen. Athens was destroyed, but the Persian navy was neatly outmanouevred by the Athenian ships at Salamis and the invasion was finally repelled by the Athenians and Spartans at the battle of Plataea.

Having proved her naval might, Athens set about creating a maritime empire, not only to increase her power but also to stabilize her combustible internal politics. She ruled the confederacy at Delos, demanding contributions from the islands in return for protection from the Persians. Sea trade became necessary to support the city's growing population, while the founding of new colonies around the Mediterranean ensured a continual food supply to Athens. The democracy became truly imperialistic under Pericles, who brought the treasure of Delos to Athens to skim off funds to rebuild and beautify the city and build the Parthenon. It was the golden age of Athens, the age of the sculptures of Phidias, the histories of Herodotos, the plays of Sophocles and Aristophanes, the philosophy of Socrates.

The main cause of the Peloponnesian War (431–404 BC) was concern over Athenian expansion in the west. Back and forth the struggle went, Sparta with superiority on land, Athens on the seas, until both city-states were near exhaustion. Finally Lysander captured Athens, razed the walls, and set up the brief rule of the Thirty Tyrants.

Although democracy and imperialism made quick recoveries (by 378 the city had set up its second Maritime League), the Peloponnesian War had struck a blow from which Athens could not totally recover. The population grew dissatisfied with public life, and refused to tolerate innovators and critics to the extent that Socrates was put to death. Economically, Athens had trouble maintaining the trade she so desperately needed. Yet her intellectual tradition held true in the 4th century, bringing forth the likes of Demosthenes, Praxiteles, Menander, Plato and Aristotle.

Philip II of Macedon took advantage of the general discontent and turmoil to bully the city-states into joining Macedon for an expedition against Persia. Athenian patriotism and independence were kept alive by the orator Demosthenes until Philip subdued the city (338). He was assassinated shortly before beginning the Persian campaign, leaving his son Alexander to conquer the East. When Alexander died, Athens had to defend herself against his striving generals, beginning with Dimitrios Poliorketes (the Besieger) who captured the city in 294. Alexandria and Pergamon became Athens' intellectual rivals, although Athens continued to be honoured by them.

In 168 BC Rome captured Athens, but gave her many privileges including the island of Delos. Eighty years later Athens betrayed Roman favour by siding with Mithridates of Pontos, for which Sulla destroyed Piraeus and the walls of the city. But Rome always remembered her cultural debt; leading Romans attended Athens' schools and gave the city great gifts. Conversely many Greek treasures ended up in Rome. St Paul came to preach to the Athenians in AD 44. In the 3rd century Goths and barbarians sacked Athens, and when they were driven away the city joined the growing Byzantine Empire.

Justinian closed the philosophy schools in AD 529 and changed the temples to churches and the Parthenon into a cathedral. By now Athens had lost almost all of her former importance. She became the plaything of the Franks after they pillaged Constantinople in 1204. St Louis appointed Guy de la Roche as Duke of Athens, a dukedom which passed through many outstretched hands: the Catalans, Neapolitans and Venetians all controlled it at various times. In 1456 the Turks took Athens, turning the Parthenon into a mosque and the Erechtheion into a harem. While attacking the Turks in 1687 Morosini and the Venetians blew up part of the Parthenon, where the Turks had stored their gunpowder. A year later the Venetians left, unsuccessful, and the citizens who had fled returned to Athens. In 1800 Lord Elgin began the large-scale removal of monuments from Athens to the British and other museums.

In 1834, after the War of Independence, Athens—then a few hundred war-scarred houses deteriorating under the Acropolis—was declared the capital of the new Greek state. Otho of Bavaria, the first King of the Greeks, brought his own architects with him and laid out a new city on the lines of Stadiou and El. Venezelou streets, which still boast most of Otho's neo-Classical public buildings. The rest of the city's architecture was abandoned to unimaginative concrete blocks, spared monotony only by the hilly Attic terrain. More and more of these hills are being pounded into villas and flats by the ubiquitous cement mixer; greater Athens squeezes in over three million lively, opiniated inhabitants (a third of the entire Greek population) who thanks to native ingenuity and EC membership are now more prosperous than they have been since the age of Pericles. Unfortunately this means a million cars now crawl the ancient streets, creating the worst smog problem east of Los Angeles, and one that threatens to choke this unique city.

Modern Athens currently has a new problem with ethnic tensions. The Gipsies have traditionally been looked on as the underclass in Greece, blamed for wrongdoings and thefts. But since thousands of impoverished refugees poured into northern Greece from Albania in 1990 they have become the new whipping boys, especially those who are not ethnically Greek. Albanians are blamed for an increase in street crime and burglaries in the cities.

Many Albanians have moved into Athens, adding to the unemployment problem in the eyes of Athenians. There has been an increase in housebreaking, theft from cars, and other crimes previously unknown in the suburbs of Athens; inevitably, the immigrants, with their visible poverty, have become the new scapegoats.

Orientation

Syntagma (or **Constitution**) **Square** is to all intents and purposes the centre of the the city, and it's here that the **Parliament Building** is to be found, backing on to the **National Gardens** and **Zappeion Park**, a haven of green and shade to escape the summer heat, with ducks to feed and a hundred benches useful for grabbing a few winks. The square itself is a busy roundabout with traffic whizzing past, but this doesn't seem to deter the people sitting feet away at the outdoor tables of the numerous overpriced cafés.

From Syntagma it's a short walk down to the far more interesting **Plaka**, the medieval centre of Athens at the foot of the Acropolis, where many of the older houses have been converted into intimate tavernas or bars, each tinkling away with its own electric bazouki. This is also a good place to look for mid-priced accommodation, and a fun part of the city to wander around in the evening.

During the day meander through Athens' nearby flea market district, to the west of **Monastiraki Square** (and metro), where bulging shops sell everything from good quality woollen goods and fake Caterpillar boots to furniture and second hand fridges. To reach the flea market, you'll find several streets en route that all claim to be the flea market, but are nothing more than tourist traps selling tat such as engraved souvenirs of Athens, fur coats, fake icons, and lots of t-shirts with 'Hellas' printed on them.

A 10-minute walk from Syntagma will take you to **Kolonaki Square**, Athens' Knightsbridge in miniature, complete with fancypants shops and restaurants (all of course expensive) and plenty of well-heeled Athenians to patronize them. Up from the square (it's a long haul on foot, but there's a funicular) is the hill of **Lycavitos**, illuminated like a fairytale tower at night. On the top sits the chapel of **St George**, a restaurant/bar and a cannon fired on national holidays. It offers the best panoramic views of Athens, including a sweeping vista down to the sea at Piraeus, *nefos* (Athens' special brand of smog) permitting.

A 20-minute walk from Syntagma, along Vass. Sofias, brings you to the Hilton Hotel, a useful landmark. Behind it are the essential Athenian neighbourhoods of **Ilissia** and **Pangrati**, the best place to get a feel for everyday life in the city. Lose yourself in their backstreets and you may find your own little taverna, of which there are plenty, rather than restrict yourself to the tourist haunts in the centre.

From Zappeion Park buses run frequently down to the coast and suburbs of **Glyfada**, **Voula** and **Vouliagmenis**. Glyfada, close to the airport, is a green and pleasant suburb, and the town itself has grown into a busy resort and a rival Kolonaki. Many smart city dwellers shop at the ritzy boutiques, and there are even a couple of well-designed (but small, fortunately) indoor shopping centres.

Here and further down the coast at Voula are pay beaches run by EOT, the National Tourist Organisation. The water is generally clean, but nothing like the more remote islands. There's also good swimming beyond Voula in the rocky coves at Vouliagmenis. Beyond Vouliagmenis, the road continues along the coast to **Sounion** and its **Temple of Poseidon** (440 BC), famous for its magnificent position and sunsets and where there's always at least one tourist searching for the column where Byron carved his name.

Agora Museum (the Theseum and Ancient Agora)

Open 8.30–3, closed Mon, adm.

The Agora was not only the market but the centre of Athenian civic and social life where citizens spent much of their day; here Socrates questioned their basic conceptions of life and law. In 480 BC the Persians destroyed all the buildings of the Agora, which were rebuilt in a much grander style; many suffered the wrath of the Romans and fires set by the barbarians. Only the foundations remain of the **Bouleuterion** or council house, and the neighbouring Temple of the Mother of the Gods, the **Metroon**, built by the Athenians in reparation for their slaying of a priest from the cult. The round **Tholos** or administration centre is where the administrators or *prytanes* worked, and as some had to be on call day and night, kitchens and sleeping quarters were included. Its final reconstruction took place after Sulla's rampage in 88 BC. Only a wall remains of the **Sanctuary of the Eponymous Heroes of Athens**, the ten who gave their names to Kleisthenes' ten tribes. The **altar of Zeus Agoraios** received the oaths of the new archons, a practice initiated by Solon.

The 4th-century **Temple of Apollo** was dedicated to the mythical father of the Ionians, who believed themselves descended from Ion, son of Apollo. The huge statue of Apollo in the Agora museum once stood inside the temple. Almost nothing remains of the **Stoa Basileios**, or of Zeus Eleutherios, which played a major role in Athenian history as the court of the annual archon, where trials concerning the security of the state took place. By the Stoa of Zeus stood the **Altar of the Twelve Gods**, from which all distances in Attica were measured. Alongside it ran the **Panathenaic Way**; some signs of its Roman rebuilding may be seen by the Church of the Holy Apostles. After crossing the Agora, this ceremonial path ascended to the Acropolis, where devotees celebrated the union of Attica. South of the Altar of Twelve Gods is the site of the Doric **Temple to Ares** (5th century BC). The **Three Giants** nearby were originally part the **Odeon of Agrippa** (15 BC); parts of the orchestra remain intact after the roof collapsed in AD 190. Confusingly, the site and the giants were reused in the façade of a 5th-century AD gymnasium, that served for a century as the site of the University of Athens until Justinian closed it down. Near the **Middle Stoa** (2nd century BC) are ruins of a **Roman temple** and the ancient shops and booths. On the other side of the Middle Stoa is the people's court, or **Heliaia**, organized by Solon in the 6th century BC to hear political questions; it remained active well into Roman times.

Between the **South and East Stoas** (2nd century BC) is the 11th-century **Church of the Holy Apostles** (Ag. Apostoli), built on the site where St Paul addressed the Athenians and restored, along with its fine paintings, in 1952. Across the Panathenaic Way run the remains of **Valerian's Wall** thrown up in AD 257 against the barbarian, its stone cannibalized from Agora buildings wrecked by the Romans. Between Valerian's Wall and the Stoa of Attalos are higgledy-piggledy ruins of the **Library of Pantainos**, built by Flavius Pantainos in AD 100 and destroyed 167 years later. Finds from the entire Agora are in the museum in the **Stoa of Attalos**, the 2nd-century BC portico built by King Attalos II of Pergamon, reconstructed by John D. Rockefeller.

The same ticket gets you into the mid-5th-century BC **Theseum**, nothing less than the best-preserved Greek temple in existence. Doric in order and dedicated to Hephaistos, the god of metals and smiths, it may well have been designed by the architect of the temple at Sounion. It is constructed almost entirely of Pentelic marble and decorated with metopes depicting the lives of Heracles and Theseus (for whom the temple was named). Converted into a church in the 5th century, it was the burial place for English Protestants until 1834, when the government declared it a national monument.

The Acropolis

Mon–Fri 8–5, Sat and Sun 8.30–3, adm.

The naturally-fortified **Acropolis** was inhabited from the end of the Neolithic Age. The Mycenaeans added a Cyclopean wall and the palace of their king. This was later replaced by a temple to the god of the spring, Poseidon, and to Athena. In mythology, these two divinities took part in a contest to decide who would be the patron of the new city. With his trident Poseidon struck the spring Klepsydra out of the rock of the Acropolis, while Athena invented the olive tree, which the Athenians judged the better trick.

The tyrant Pisistratos ordered a great gate constructed in the wall, but Delphi cursed it and the Athenians dismantled it. In 480 BC the temple's cult statue of Athena was hurried to the protection of Salamis, just before the Persians burnt the Acropolis. Themistocles built a new rampart out of the old Parthenon, and under Perikles the present plan of the Acropolis buildings was laid out.

The path to the Acropolis follows the Panathenaic Way, laid out at the consecration of the Panathenaic Festival in 566 BC. The Acropolis entrance is defended by the **Beulé Gate** (named after Ernest Beulé, the archaeologist who found it); the monumental stairways were built by the Romans and the two lions are from Venice. The reconstructed Panathenaic ramp leads to the equally reconstructed

Propylaia, the massive gateway replacing Pisistratos' cursed gate, built by Pericles' architect Mnesikles. The ancient Greeks considered the Proplyaia the architectural equal of the Parthenon itself, although it was never completed because of the Peloponnesian War. On either side of the Propylaia's entrance are two wings; the north held a picture gallery (Pinakotheke) while the smaller one to the south consisted of only one room of an unusual shape, because the priests of the neighbouring Nike temple didn't want the wing in their precinct. The original entrance had five doors, the central one pierced by the Panathenaic Way.

Temple of Athena Nike

The Ionic Temple of Athena Nike, or *Wingless Victory*, was built by the architect Kallikrates in 478 BC of Pentelic marble. Inside was kept the cult statue of Athena, a copy of a much older wooden statue. Its lack of wings, unlike later victory statues, gave it its second name. In 1687 the Turks destroyed the temple to build a tower. It was rebuilt in 1835 and again in 1936, when the bastion beneath it threatened to crumble away. The north and western friezes were taken to England by Lord Elgin and have been replaced by cement casts. From the temple of Athena Nike the whole Saronic Gulf could be seen in the pre-smog days, and it was here that Aegeus watched for the return of his son Theseus from his Cretan adventure with the Minotaur. Theseus was to have signalled his victory with a white sail but forgot; at the sight of the black sail of death, Aegeus threw himself off the precipice in despair.

The Parthenon

The Parthenon, the glory of the Acropolis and probably the most famous building in the world, if not the most imitated, is a Doric temple constructed between 447 and 432 BC under the direction of Phidias, the greatest artist and sculptor of the Periclean age. Originally called the Great Temple, it took the name Parthenon (Chamber of Virgins) a hundred years after its completion. Constructed entirely of Pentelic marble, it originally held Phidias' famous statue of Athena Parthenos, more than 36ft high and made of ivory and gold. Look closely, and you'll see that the Parthenon's foundation is curved slightly to prevent an illusion of drooping caused by straight horizontals. To make the columns appear straight the architect bent them a few centimetres inward. Corner columns were made wider to complete the illusion of perfect form.

The outer colonnade consists of 46 columns and above them are the remnants of the Doric frieze left behind by the beaverish Lord Elgin: the east side portrayed the battle of giants and gods, the south the Lapiths and Centaurs (mostly in the

British Museum today), on the west the Greeks and the Amazons, and on the north the battle of Troy. Little remains of the pediment sculptures of the gods. Above the interior colonnade, the masterful Ionic frieze designed by Phidias himself shows the quadrennial Panathenaic Procession in which Athena was brought a golden crown and a new sacred garment, or *peplos*.

The Parthenon's roof was blown sky high in 1687 when a Venetian bomb hit the Turks' powder stores inside; the destruction was continued in 1894 by an earthquake and today the nefarious *nefos* smog threatens to give the kiss of death to this graceful prototype of a thousand bank buildings. Entrance within the Parthenon itself is forbidden, to save on wear and tear. What is intriguing—and sometimes you can see the work in progress—is that after all these years the Greek government has decided to pick up all the pieces lying scattered since Morosini's day, and reconstruct as much of the temple as possible.

The Erechtheion

The last great monument on the Acropolis is the Erechtheion, a peculiar Ionic temple that owes its idiosyncrasies to the various cult items and the much older sanctuary it was built to encompass. Beneath the temple stood the Mycenaean House of Erechtheus, mentioned by Homer, and the primitive cult sanctuary of Athena; on one side of this grew the Sacred Olive Tree created by Athena, while under the north porch was the mark left by Poseidon's trident when he brought forth the divine spring. The tomb of Kekrops, the legendary founder of Athens, is in the Porch of the Maidens or Caryatids, where Erechtheus died at the hand of either Zeus or Poseidon. Within the temple stood the ancient cult statue of Athena Polias, endowed with the biggest juju of them all, solemnly dressed in the sacred *peplos* and crown.

After the Persian fires, the sanctuary was quickly restored, but the marble temple planned by Pericles was not begun until 421 BC. Used as a church in the 7th century, it became a harem under the Turks, who used the sacred place of the trident marks as a toilet. Lord Elgin nicked parts of this temple as well, including one of the caryatids which you can now see in the British Museum; acidic air pollution has forced the Greek government to replace the other girls with casts.

Basically the Erechtheion is a rectangular building with three porches. Inside were two cellas, or chambers: the East Cella dedicated to Athena Polias, the smaller to Poseidon–Erechtheus. Six tall Ionic columns mark the north porch where the floor and roof were cut away to reveal Poseidon's trident marks, for it was sacrilegious to hide something so sacred from the view of the gods. The six famous maidens gracefully supporting the roof on their heads are another Ionian motif.

The Acropolis Museum

(open Tues–Fri 8–4.30, Mon 10–4.30, Sat and Sun 8.30–2.30)

The museum houses sculptures and reliefs from the temples, in particular the Erechtheion's maidens, or Kores. But frankly, the museum's contents are far less impressive than the site outside, unless you're a scholar of classics or have a big interest in archaeology.

Below the Acropolis is the **Areopagos**, or hill of Ares, the god of war. There sat the High Council, who figured so predominantly in Aeschylos' play *The Eumenides* where mercy defeated vengeance for the first time in history during the trial of the matricide Orestes. Although Pericles removed much of the original power of the High Council, under the control of the ex-archons it continued to advise on the Athenian constitution for hundreds of years.

The Theatres

*Prices vary: 800 dr. is the current rate of admission to the site of The **Acropolis**, for an adult without a concession.*

On the south side of the Acropolis are two theatres. The older, the **Theatre of Dionysos**, was used from the 6th century BC when Thespis created the first true drama, and was continually modified up to the time of Nero. In this theatre the annual Greater Dionysia was held, in honour of the god of wine and patron divinity of the theatre, Dionysos. The dramatic competitions led to the premières of some of the world's greatest tragedies. The stage that remains is from the 4th century BC, while the area before the stage; the **proskenion**, is decorated with 1st century AD scenes based on the life of Dionysos. Beside the theatre stood two temples to Dionysos Eleutherios.

Above the theatre is an **Asklepieion**, a sanctuary to the god of healing. The stoa which remains is from the second rebuilding, while the first and oldest sanctuary to the west first belonged to a water goddess, but very little of it remains. Both the old and new Asklepieions were connected with the parent cult at Epidauros.

The **Theatre of Herodes Atticus** was built and named for the Rockefeller of his day in AD 161 and originally partially covered. Now it hosts the annual mid-May and September **Festival of Athens**, where the cultures of modern Europe and ancient Greece are combined in theatre, ballet, and classical music concerts performed by companies from all over the world.

Other Museums

Benaki Museum: On the corner of Vassilis Sofias and Koumbari St, *open 8.30–3, daily.* This museum holds the collection of Antonios Benaki, who spent 35 years amassing objects from Europe and Asia, Byzantine and Islamic. The Byzantine artworks (6th–14th centuries) are fascinating examples of early Christian art: icons, jewellery, ceramics, silver and embroidery, while the post-Byzantine exhibits (15th–17th century) show the influences of Islamic and Italian art. There are two icons by the Cretan-born El Greco, painted before his departure to Venice and Spain—the *Adoration of the Magi* (1560–65) and the *Evangelist Luke* (1560). The section on folk art, dating from the Ottoman occupation, contains a superb collection of costumes and artefacts from the Ionian islands to Cyprus.

National Archaeology Museum: Patission and Tossitsa Sts, *open 8–5, Sat and Sun 8.30–3, Mon 11–5, free Thurs and Sun.* The National Museum contains some of the most spectacular ancient Greek art anywhere—the Minoan-style frescoes from Santorini, gold from Mycenae (including the famous mask of Agamemnon), statues, reliefs, tomb stelae, and ceramics and vases from every period. The Cycladic collection includes one of the first known musicians of the Greek world, the sculpture of the little harpist that has become the virtual symbol of the Cyclades. The star of the sculpture rooms is a virile bronze of Poseidon (5th-century BC) about to launch his trident, found off the coast of Evia in 1928; around him are some outstanding archaic Kouros statues and the Stele of Hegeso, an Athenian beauty, enveloped by the delicate folds of her robe, seated on a throne. The museum has a shop on the lower level, with reproductions of exhibits by expert craftsmen, so accurate that each piece is issued with a certificate declaring it an authentic fake so you can take it out of the country.

National Gallery: 50 Vass. Konstantinou, across from the Athens Hilton, *open 9–3, Sun 10–2, closed Mon.* Also known as the Alexander Soustou Museum, the National Gallery concentrates on art by modern Greek artists. Works by the leading contemporary painter, Nikos Hadzikyriakos-Ghikas, are permanently displayed on the ground floor, while the lower level is used for rotating exhibitions. The museum shop has posters, cards, catalogues and jewellery, and there's a pleasant outdoor café, for when you've done the rounds.

Historical and Ethnological Museum: At the Palea Vouli (Old Parliament), Stadiou St, *open 9–1, closed Mon.* This imposing neo-Classical edifice is the guardian of Greek history, from the fall of Constantinople to the present day. The bronze warrior on horseback is Theodoros Kolokotronis, hero of the War of Independence, while exhibits within trace the history of modern Greece in paintings, sculptures, armaments (including Byron's sword and helmet), maps, folk costumes, jewellery and more covering every period, from Ottoman rule to resistance against the Nazis in 1940.

Popular Art Museum: 17 Kydathinaion St, *open 10–2, closed Mon.* The museum has a collection of Greek folk art, both religious and secular, along with paintings by naïve artists.

The Pnyx: On the hill west of the Acropolis. The Pnyx once hosted the General Assembly of Athens and the great speeches of Pericles and Demosthenes. On assembly days citizens were literally rounded up to fill the minimum attendance quota of 5000, but they were paid for their services to the state. Later the assembly was transferred to the theatre of Dionysos. On the summit of the nearby Hill of the Muses is the **Philopappos Monument**, the tomb of Caius Julius Antiochos Philopappos, a Syrian Prince and citizen of Athens. The monument was built for him by the Athenians in AD 114 in gratitude for his beneficence to the city.

Roman Agora: Located between the Agora and the Acropolis, *open 8.30–3pm closed Mon. Adm 1000dr.* Dating from the end of the Hellenistic age, the Roman Agora contains the celebrated **Tower of the Winds**, or Clock of Andronikos, built in the 1st century BC. Run by a hydraulic mechanism, it stayed open day and night so that the citizens could know the time. Its name comes from the frieze of the eight winds that decorate its eight sides, although it has lost its ancient bronze Triton weathervane. The Roman Agora also contains the **Gate of Athena Archegetis**, built by money sent over from Julius and Augustus Caesar; there is also a court and the ruins of stoae. Beside the Agora is the Fehiye Camii, the Victory or Corn Market Mosque.

Byzantine Museum: 22 Vassilis Sofias, *open 8.30–3, closed Mon.* This monumental collection of religious treasures and paintings dates from the Early Byzantine period to the 19th century—not only icons but marble sculptures, mosaics, woodcarvings, frescoes, manuscripts and ecclesiastical robes. There are three rooms on the ground floor arranged as chapels, one Early Christian, another Middle Byzantine, and the third post-Byzantine.

Museum of Cycladic Art: 4 Neoforos Douka St (between Byzantine and Benaki museums), *open 10–3.30, Sat 10–2.30, closed Tues and Sun.* This museum houses a vast collection of Cycladic figurines and objects dating back to 3200–2000 BC, illustrating everyday life. The female figurines with folded arms are unique. The newest addition is the 'Treasure of Keros', a small island near Naxos where excavations in the 1950s and 60s unearthed a wealth of figurines.

Keramikos and Museum: 148 Ermou St, *open 8.30–3, closed Mon.* The ancient cemetery or Keramikos was used for burials from the 12th century BC into Roman times, but the most impressive and beautiful finds are in the rich private tombs built by the Athenians in the 4th century BC. Large stone vases mark the graves of the unmarried dead, while others are in the form of miniature temples and stelae; the best are in the National Museum.

Temple of Olympian Zeus: Olgas and Amalias Avenues, *open 8.30–3, closed Mon.* Fifteen columns recall what Livy called 'the only temple on earth of a size adequate to the greatness of the god'. The foundations were laid by the tyrant Pisistratos, but work ground to a halt with the fall of his dynasty, only to be continued in 175 BC by a Roman architect, Cossutius. It was half finished when Cossutius' patron, Antiochos IV of Syria kicked the bucket, leaving the Emperor Hadrian to complete it in AD 131. Nearby are the ruins of ancient houses and a bath and at the far end stands **Hadrian's Arch**, neatly dividing the city of Theseus from the city of Hadrian. The Athenians traditionally come here to celebrate the Easter Resurrection.

Museum of the City of Athens: Plateia Klafthmonos, *open Mon, Wed, Fri, Sat 9–1.30; free Wed.* Located in the re-sited neo-Classical palace of King Otho, this new museum contains photos, memorabilia and a model showing Athens as it was soon after it became the capital of modern Greece.

Byzantine Churches and Monasteries in Athens

Agii Theodori: This 11th-century church in Klafthmonos Square at the end of Dragatsaniou St is most notable for its beautiful door; the bell tower and some of the decorations inside are more recent additions.

Kapnikarea: A few blocks from Agii Theodori, on Ermou St. Tiny Kapnikarea (the chapel of the University of Athens) was built in the late 11th century in the shape of a Greek cross, its central cupola sustained by four columns with Roman capitals.

Panayia Gorgoepikoos (or Ag. Eleftherios): Situated in Mitropoleos Square and known as the little Metropolitan to distinguish it from the nearby cathedral, this is the loveliest church in Athens. Built in the 12th century almost entirely of ancient marbles the builders found lying around; note the ancient calendar of state festivals embedded over the door. Curiously, the **Cathedral** (just to the north) was built in 1840–55 with the same collage technique, using bits and pieces from 72 destroyed churches.

Dafni and its Wine Festival: 10 km from Athens; take bus 282 from Eleftherios Square. The name Dafni derives from the temple of Apollo Dafneios (of the laurel), built near the Sacred Way. The site became a walled monastery in the 6th century and in 1080 a new church was built, decorated with the best Byzantine mosaics in southern Greece. These are dominated in the vault of the dome by the tremendous figure of Christ Pantokrator 'the all powerful', his eyes spellbinding and tragic, 'as though He were in flight from an appalling doom' as Patrick Leigh Fermor has written. From mid-August until September, daily 7.45pm–12.30am, the monastery park holds a festival with over 60 different Greek wines (free once you've paid the 300 dr. admission at the gate) accompanied by (poor and over-priced) food, singing and dancing, an event well-attended by Athenians and visitors alike.

(01–)   *Where to Stay in Athens*

Athens is a big noisy city, especially so at night when you want to sleep—unless you do as the Greeks do and take a long afternoon siesta. Piraeus (*see* below) may be a better bet, no less noisy but much more convenient for catching those up-at-the-crack-of-dawn ships to the islands, although women on their own may find too many sailors and working girls about to feel at ease. All accommodation fills up quickly in the summer and if you don't have a reservation, or erratic boat schedules have mangled your booking, it's best to head straight for the EOT office on Syntagma Square (in the National Bank building) and use their hotel finding service.

luxury

New luxury chain hotels are mushrooming up everywhere just outside the city centre—there's the **Ledra Marriott** at 113–115 Syngrou, © 934 7711, fax 935 8603, featuring a Chinese–Japanese restaurant, and a hydrotherapy pool you can soak in with a view of the Parthenon. Another addition to the scene (and one on a human scale) is the 76-room **Astir Palace Athens Hotel** on Syntagma Square, © 364 3112, fax 364 2825 owned by the National Bank of Greece. While it was under construction, ancient foundations and waterpipes were uncovered and these are incor-porated into the décor of the hotel's restaurant, the **Apokalypsis**, located below street level (Greek and international cuisine). Despite its location, specially insulated glass windows keep out the hubbub below the rooms. There's a sauna, and each room features a mini bar and colour TV (with an in-house movie channel).

Directly across the square from the Astir is the **Grande Bretagne**, ✆ 323 0251, fax 322 8034 originally built in 1862 to house members of the Greek royal family who couldn't squeeze into the main palace (the current Parliament building) up the square. The Grande Bretagne is the only 'grand' hotel in Greece worthy of the description, with a vast marble lobby, elegant rooms (now air conditioned and appointed with such modern conveniences as direct dial phones and colour TV), a formal dining room, and an appearance of grandeur and style that the newer hotels, with all their plushness, may never achieve. Having said that, on our most recent stay there (Autumn 1993) we found the service to be positively complacent, which is disappointing at the prices they charge. Even if you're not going to stay there, you may want to poke your head in (there's a pleasant bar) to see where the crowned heads of Europe lodge in Athens—and where the Nazis set up their headquarters during the Second World War. Winston Churchill spent Christmas 1944 at the Grande Bretagne and was lucky to escape a bomb meant for him, planted in the hotel's complex sewer system.

On a less exalted level, but with a far more fetching view is the **Royal Olympic Hotel** at 28 Diakou, ✆ 922 6411, fax 923 3317, facing the Temple of Olympian Zeus and Mt Lycavitos. Rooms here are American in spirit, with a number of family-sized suites, and if you have the misfortune to get a room without a view, there's the wonderful panorama from the rooftop bar.

expensive

The **Electra Palace** at 18 Nikodimou St, ✆ 324 1401, fax 324 1875, has views of the Acropolis and a wonderful rooftop swimming pool in a garden setting—something you don't find every day in Athens. Rooms are air conditioned and there's a garage adjacent to the hotel. Half-board is obligatory—unfortunately, because the hotel is quite close to the good tavernas of Plaka. More reasonable, and centrally located just off Syntagma Square, the **Astor**, 16 Karagiorgi Servias, ✆ 325 5555, also has fully air conditioned rooms and a rooftop garden restaurant.

moderate

The best value in this category (and a big favourite with Americans) has long been the **Hotel Alkistis** at 18 Plateia Theatrou, ✆ 321 9811, all rooms with private baths and phones, all very modern and perfectly clean. If the Alkistis is full, a good second bet is the **Hotel Museum** at

16 Bouboulinas St, ✆ 360 5611, right at the back of the Archaeology Museum. The rooms are about the same, but the prices are a bit higher. **Hotel Tempi**, 29 Eolou St, ✆ 321 3175, near Monastiraki, is more downgrade, but is cheaper and has washing facilities. **Art Gallery** at Erekhthiou 5, Veikou, ✆ 923 8376, is a pleasant place at the lower end of this price category, though it is out of the centre; Plaka is a 20-minute walk, more if you're fumbling with a map.

cheap

Most of the inexpensive hotels are around Plaka. For better or worse, the government has shut down many of the old dormitory houses that grew up in the 1960s to contain the vanguard of mass tourism in Greece— every hippy in Europe, or at least so it seemed to the amazed Greeks. Survivors of the government purge have upgraded themselves but are still a bargain—and many still let you sleep on the roof for a thousand drachmas (not an unpleasant option in the thick heat of August). Best bets in the cheaper category include:

Hotel Phaedra, 16 Herefondos St, ✆ 323 8461, just off Filellinon St, with free hot showers; unreconstructed pre-war interior, and pleasant staff (double room 6000dr, more in season).

John's Place, 5 Patroou St, ✆ 322 9719. Around 4000dr.

Hotel Cleo, 3 Patroou St, ✆ 322 9053, small and near Plaka.

Student Inn, 16 Kidathineon, ✆ 324 4808, very conveniently placed in the Plaka, and ideal for the rowdy younger crowd (1.30am curfew though).

Joseph's House, 13 Markou Botsari, ✆ 923 1204, in a quieter area on the south side of the Acropolis; washing facilities available (take advantage of it—if you're travelling in the islands for any length of time, washing clothes will be your biggest headache).

Less savoury, but also less expensive is the city's **IYHF Youth Hostel**, inconveniently located far from the centre at 57 Kypselis St, Kypseli, ✆ (01) 822 5860. A better option, though it is not a member of the YHA, is the **Student's Hostel** at 75 Damareos St, Pangrati, ✆ 751 9530. The nearest **campsites** to Athens are at Dafni Monastery, and down on the coast at Voula. When your make you way through the metro station at Piraeus, you're guaranteed to have fliers thrust in your hand for other rock-bottom options.

Athenians rarely dine out before 10 or 11pm, and they want to be
entertained afterwards. If it's warm, chances are they'll drive out to the
suburbs or the sea shore. **Glyfada**, near the airport, is a popular destination and on a summer evening the cool sea breeze can be a life saver after
the oppressive heat of Athens. The obvious meal to choose is something
from the sea, and most of the tavernas specialize in fish (especially red
mullet, or *barbounia*), lobster, squid and shrimp, although, as everywhere
in Greece, it's the most expensive food you can order. Remember that
prices marked for fish usually indicate how much per kilo, not per
portion.

Glyfada

Leading off the main square in Glyfada is a street almost entirely devoted
to excellent restaurants and friendly, inexpensive bars. At reasonably
priced **George's**, the steak will be cooked according to your specifica-
tions and the meatballs (*keftedes*) are a speciality. To feed the large
foreign community in Glyfada, a plethora of fast food joints has grown up
in the area, and now expensive Arab restaurants (complete with imported
Middle Eastern singers and belly dancers) have made an appearance on
the scene.

central Athens

Costayiannis, 37 Zaimi, near the National Archaeology Museum, with a
succulent display of food in the glass cabinets near the entrance preparing
you for a memorable culinary evening. Apart from the superb seafood, the
'ready food' is unbeatable—try the quail with roast potatoes, the roast
pork in wine and herb sauce or the rabbit *stifado*, accompanied by barrelled retsina, if you've developed a taste for it. Prices here are very
reasonable—3500 dr. for a full evening meal (closed lunchtimes and Sundays). As near to a traditional taverna that you'll find, the **Taverna
Karavitis** is a few streets up from the old Olympic stadium, on the corner
of Arkitinou and Pafsaniou and housed in a long, low white building, with
barrels lining the walls. Athenians come here for a good time; the food,
served by friendly young lads in jeans, is better than average, wine
is served from the barrel, and it's open till late (1500 dr.). Just off
Mikalakopoulou St, and not far from the Hilton Hotel is **John's Village
(To Chorio tou Yianni)**, a cut above the ordinary taverna and warmly

decorated with hand-woven rugs and island pottery. The accompanying music, played by a strolling minstrel, makes this a favourite spot to spend an evening without breaking the bank. There's a good variety of well-prepared dishes and a meal will cost about 3000 dr. Behind the Hilton, on Mikalakopoulou, is the Cypriot restaurant **Othello's**, with delicious, authentic cuisine at around 2500 dr. for a meal.

the Plaka

Plaka is the place to head for for pleasant restaurants and *al fresco* dining in the evening. There are scores of places catering for the passing tourist trade, and they are all very competent, though few serve true, vernacular food that you'll find on the islands (if you make the effort to look for it). Despite this, the Plaka is still the perennial favourite with both Greeks and tourists. The atmosphere at night is exciting with its crowded tavernas perched precariously on uneven steps, Greek dancers whirling and leaping on stages the size of postage stamps, light bulbs flashing and *bouzouki* music filling the air. A typical charming Plaka taverna is the rooftop **Thespes**, 100 m along from the Plaka Square, where a selection of starters, such as *tzatziki*, *taramasalata* and fried aubergine (eggplant) followed by lamb chops and plenty of wine won't cost you much more than 2000 dr. In some of the other tavernas you may not be as lucky and will have to pay well over the odds, particularly if there's live music, for food that rarely rises above the mediocre. One other outstanding exception is **Platanos**, the oldest taverna in the Plaka, near the Tower of the Four Winds. The food here is good and wholesome, but forget about perusing the menu—it's definitely an 'in the kitchen and point' joint, and inexpensive at 1500–2000 dr. for a meal. In the heart of Plaka, in Filomosou Square, where every visitor lands up sooner or later, you can eat well at **O Costas** or **Xynou Taverna**, 4 Geronda St, which serves excellent food in a garden setting, with strolling musicians playing traditional Greek music. It's very popular (closed on Sat and Sun), and reservations are a must (© 322 1065; 2500 dr.). Off touristy Adrianou St, with all its souvenirs, the family-run taverna **Tsegouras**, 2 Epicharmou, is in a walled garden in the shade of an enormous gum tree, with good Greek food for around 2000 dr.

While walking around Plaka, you're likely to pass **Brettos**, a small but colourfully-lit shop selling own-label *mastika* and liqueurs; try some, it beats bringing back a bottle of ouzo with you on the aeroplane.

around the Plaka

Just outside the Plaka, two blocks south of Hadrian's arch at 5 Lembessi St, **O Kouvelos** is another typical, reliable Athenian taverna, serving excellent *meze* and barrelled retsina. They'll save you the bother of ordering the meze by planting it on the table in front of you; don't be shy to change it if you want something different (2000 dr.) In the same area (cross Makriyianni St), you could try **Socrates Prison**, 20 Mitseon St, a real favourite with locals and expats. Greek food with a flair in attractive surroundings, though the service can be variable. Bottled or barrelled wine (2000 dr., evenings only, closed Sun). A few blocks west of here, at 7 Garivaldi St, the **Greek House** has dining on a rooftop terrace with a most beautiful view of the Acropolis. Don't be put off by the name; this restaurant serves superb and reasonably priced specialities—try the 'Virginia', slices of *filet mignon* with mushrooms, or the shrimp salad. They also make wonderful spinach and cheese pies (2500 dr.). Near the Monastiraki *elektriko* (underground) station, search out **Taverna Sigalas**, a bustling place where you can soak up the least pretentious side of Athenian life; usual Greek food served at unpredictable temperatures, and Greek folk music to make you feel you never want to go home (1500–2000 dr.).

around Omonia Square

Omonia Square is a great place to try Greek street food. You can buy bags of nuts, coconut sweets, savoury pies (*tyropitta*—cheese, and *spanako-pitta*—spinach), late-night souvlaki, and sandwiches, and it's all very cheap. Near Omonia Square are a number of cheap restaurants displaying cuts of roast lamb, pork and the occasional grinning sheep's head. They're really worth a try if you are watching your drachme, but feel like a 'proper' meal—a portion of chicken with rubber fried spuds and a small bottle of retsina will set you back about 1000 dr. Of the half-a-dozen or so places, try **Platanos** on Satombriandou.

ethnic cuisine

Athens is well supplied with ethnic eating places—French, Italian, Spanish, Chinese, Japanese, Mexican, American and restaurants of other nationalities are scattered around the capital. Of particular note for lovers of German food is the **Rittenburg** at 11 Formionos in Pangrati, where the boiled and grilled sausages, and pork with sauerkraut are tops. North German dishes are on the menu in the small, intimate and aptly named

Delicious in Kolonaki at 6 Zalokosta—marinated fish, *bratkartoffeln*, lovely goulash and home-made black bread (2500 dr.). Asian restaurants are all relatively expensive. The Chinese-Malaysian **Rasa Sayang**, in the seaside suburb of Glyfada, on Palea Leoforos Vouliagmenis and 2 Kiou, serves great Peking Duck and beef with mango slices, among many other items (3000 dr.). A little further down the coast at Voula, **Loon Fung Tien** does fixed-price *dim sum* (buffet) lunchtimes on Sunday. Italian restaurants are established in every major European city, and Athens is no exception. **Boschetto**, in the Evangelismos Gardens opposite the Hilton, is one of the city's best. Exquisite spaghetti with *frutti di mare*, inventive main courses (guinea hen with bacon and pomegranate sauce) and fine desserts (4000 dr.). In Kolonaki the trendy **Pane e Vino**, 8 Spefsipou, is popular for its antipasti (aubergine and Gorgonzola rolls) and pasta (tagliolini with smoked salmon), together with main dishes such as sole with mussels or scaloppine with prosciutto (4–5000 dr.) A collection of top class, expensive French restaurants have graced the Athens culinary scene for years. In Kolonaki **Je Reviens**, 49 Xenokratous, is an old favourite, with live music and outdoor seating (5000 dr.). Near the American Embassy **Balthazar**, 27 Tsoha and Vournazou, is a renovated mansion with an attractive bar and a comprehensive selection of international dishes, but it's best to book ✆ 644 1215; 3500 dr.

hotel restaurants

Some of the luxury hotels in Athens have some swish theme restaurants (with swish prices of course). The **Ledra Marriott** (p.81) has the 'Polynesian' **Kona Kai** in an exotic tropical setting, with all the delicacies from that other island paradise; a few blocks down, the **Athenaeum Intercontinental** also has Asian cuisine in its **Kublai Khan** restaurant.

Bars

Watering holes abound in Athens, many of them serving bar food, and most of the English-speaking community do the rounds of the **Red Lion**, the **Underground** and the **Ploughman's**, all within a stone's throw of the Hilton.

Wine bars are a fairly recent addition to Athens' nightlife. If you want to try some finer wines from Greece and Europe, the following places will oblige: **Kelari**, in the Hilton, serving Greek dishes as an accompaniment, in a friendly, warm décor; **Loutro**, 18 Feron, way north near Victoria

Square, decorated in sophisticated Roman bath style, serving imaginative dishes to accompany the French, Italian and lesser known Greek wines; **Le Sommelier d'Athènes**, Leof. Kifissias in Kifissia, in a beautiful old suburban villa, with an emphasis on French and Italian; **Strofilia**, 7 Karitsi (behind the Historical Museum), with mainly Greek labels, and an extensive salad bar.

Piraeus

The port of Athens, Piraeus—pronounced 'Pirefs'—was the greatest port of the ancient world and remains today one of the busiest in the Mediterranean. In Greece, a country that derives most of its livelihood from the sea in one way or another, Piraeus is the true capital, while Athens is a mere sprawling suburb where the bureaucrats live. Still, it takes a special visitor to find much charm in the tall grey buildings and dusty hurly-burly in the streets, although Marina Zea and Mikrolimani with their yachts, brightly-lit tavernas and bars are a handsome sight, as are the neon signs flashing kinetically as you sail to or from Piraeus in the evening. The tall, half-finished building on the waterfront was built and abandoned by the junta when they found that the foundations were mixed with sea water. Somehow its useless silhouette makes a fitting monument to that ignorant and often cruel government.

An Historical Outline

Themistocles founded the port of Piraeus in the 5th century BC when Phaliron, Athens' ancient port, could no longer meet the growing needs of the city. From the beginning Piraeus was cosmopolitan and up-to-date: the Miletian geometrician Hippodamos laid it out in a straight grid of streets that have changed little today. The centre of action was always the huge agora in the middle of the city. Under its stoae the world's first commercial fairs and trade expositions were held, some on an international scale. All religions were tolerated, and women were allowed for the first time to work outside the home.

As Piraeus was so crucial to Athens' power, the conquering Spartan Lysander destroyed the famous Long Walls that linked city and port in 404, at the end of the Peloponnesian War. Piraeus made a brief comeback under Konon and Lykurgos, who rebuilt its arsenals. After the 100-year Macedonian occupation and a period of peace, Sulla decimated the city to prevent any anti-Roman resistance, and for 1900 years Piraeus dwindled away into an insignificant village with a population as low as 20, even losing its name to become Porto Leone (after an ancient lion statue, carved from runes by Harald Hadraada and his Vikings in 1040 and carted off by Morosini as a trophy to embellish Venice's Arsenal). Since the selection of Athens as the capital of independent Greece, Piraeus has regained its former glory as the reigning port of a sea-going nation.

Getting Around

In Piraeus this usually means getting out of town as quickly as possible. **Ships** are grouped according to their destination and almost anyone you ask will be able to tell you the precise location of any vessel. The cluster of ticket agents around the port is very noisy and competitive, but prices to the islands are fixed, so the only reason to shop around is to see if there is an earlier or faster ship to the island of your choice. Beware that ticket agents often don't know or won't tell you information on lines other than the ones they carry. Only the Tourist Police on Akti Miaouli have complete information on boat schedules.

There are three **railway stations.** The half-underground Elektriko serves Athens as far north as the posh suburb of Kifissia, setting off every 10 minutes from 6am to 1.30am from the terminal opposite the quay. Stations for northern Greece and for the Peloponnese are further down the road.

Buses to Athens run day and night, the main 'Green' line (no. 040) taking you directly to Syntagma Square. The express line no. 19 bus service to East and West Airport leaves from Karaiskaki Square.

Tourist Police

Akti Miaouli, ✆ 452 3670.
Irron Politechniou, ✆ 412 0325.

The Sights

If you find yourself in Piraeus with time to kill on a Sunday morning, take a prowl through the flea market parallel to the underground (Elektriko) line, where you may well happen across some oddity brought back by a Greek Sinbad. If culture beckons, there's an **Archaeology Museum** at 31 Har. Trikoupi St, with an above average collection of antiquities (*8.30–3, closed Mon*), or perhaps the **Maritime Museum** on Akti Themistocles by Freatidos St, with intriguing plans of Greece's greatest naval battles, ship models and mementoes from the War of Independence (*8.30–1, closed Sun and Mon*). The **Hellenistic Theatre** at Zea occasionally has performances in the summer.

Beaches are not far away, although the sea isn't exactly sparkling and on most you must pay. Kastella is the closest, followed by New Phaliron which is free. Buses go to Ag. Kosmos by the airport, where you can play tennis or volleyball; at Glyfada, further down the road, there's more wholesome swimming and a golf course for duffers.

Zea, Glyfada and Vouliagmeni are the three **marinas** organized by the National Tourist Organization. Piraeus is also the place to charter yachts or sail boats, from 12-foot dinghies to deluxe twin-screw yachts, if you've missed your island connection (*see* yachting pp. 17–22).

Where to Stay in Piraeus

Hotel accommodation in Piraeus is geared towards businessmen, and unfortunately less so towards people who have arrived on a late-night ship or plan to depart on an early morning one. Brave souls sleep out in the squares, particularly in Karaiskaki, but they have to put up with lights, noise, the neighbouring discotheques and sailors of every nationality who hang around hoping for something to happen.

expensive

If you're with the kids, try the quiet and very clean **Hotel Anemoni**, at Karaoli Demetriou and Evripidou 65–67, © 413 6881; since it's not directly on the port you miss the sailors and some of the racket. All rooms are air conditioned, and there's a free transfer service to the port.

moderate

If you want to be within walking distance of the docks, the **Hotel Triton**, © 417 3457, is one of the best of the many in the area; its B class doubles start at 5500 dr., but go shooting up in high summer. All rooms have private bath and breakfast is available. A mediocre alternative is the **Ideal**, 142 Notara St, © 451 1727, 50 m from the customs house, with air conditioning and private bath.

cheap

On the lower end of the scale there are many D & E class hotels, some of which are not as appetizing as they might be, but their rates range from 3000 dr. to around 5000 dr. Typical of these is **Achillion**, 63 Notara St, © 412 4029.

Around the port the fare is generally fast food and giro spinners, while the tavernas are so greasy it's a wonder they don't slide off the street. For seafood (especially if you're on an expense account), the bijou little harbour of Mikrolimano (or Turkolimano) is the traditional place to go, although too many tourists with too much money have inflated the price to a nasty pitch. A far better idea is to forego fish and eat up at the excellent **Kaliva** in Vass. Pavlou, Kastella, with a splendid view down over the harbour (excellent meat dinners for 2500 dr.) followed by a stroll through Mikrolimano for a coffee and Metaxa on the harbour front. But if it's fish you must have, head over to Frates, around from the Zea Marina yacht harbour, where several moderately-priced places offer fresh fish and sea views. There's really not all that much to distinguish one from another; just stroll around until you find a fish that winks at you. Zea Marina itself is a vast necklace of neon, where the locals haunt the inexpensive **American Pizza**, but there are places with Greek pizza and other fare, both on the harbour and on the streets giving into it.

If you've got time between boats or flights, the stretch of coast between Piraeus and the airport has a few possibilities. Chefs from the eastern Mediterranean are undoubtedly the kings of kebab; try the **Adep Kebab**, 20 Leof. Possidonos in Paleo Phaliron, where the meat is delicately flavoured with the spices of the Levant. Specialities are the *adana* kebab, *domatesli* kebab (cooked with tomatoes on charcoal) and the succulent shish-kebab, marinated in milk, lemon juice, oil and spices. Alternatively, in Nea Smyrni, the **Tria Asteria**, 7 Melitos and 77 Plastira, is run by Armenians from Istanbul. The choice of appetizers is endless, including delicious *cli kofte*, a meatball of veal and lamb, bulgur wheat and pine nuts. This is also the only place in Athens to find *tandir* kebab, lamb which has been smoked and then baked in a red wine sauce. At either of these restaurants, count on around 3000 dr.

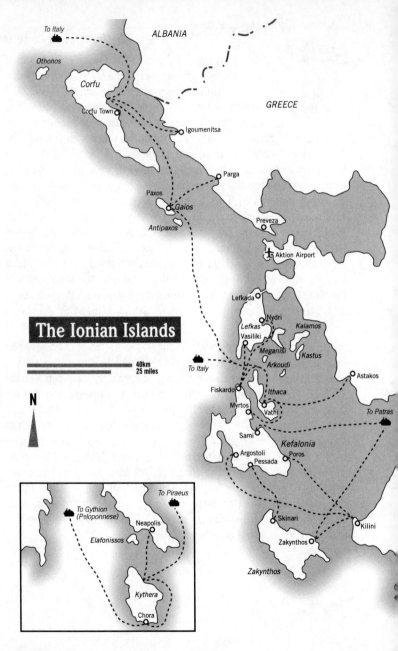

The Ionian Islands

40km
25 miles

N

To Italy

ALBANIA

GREECE

Othonos

Corfu

Corfu Town

Igoumenitsa

Parga

Paxos

Gaios

Antipaxos

Preveza

Aktion Airport

Lefkada

Nydri

Lefkas

Vasiliki

Kalamos

Meganisi

Kastus

Arkoudi

To Italy

Fiskardo

Ithaca

Myrtos

Vathi

Astakos

Sami

Kefalonia

Argostoli

Poros

Pessada

To Patras

Skinari

Kilini

Zakynthos

Zakynthos

To Piraeus

To Gythion
(Peloponnese)

Neapolis

Elafonissos

Kythera

Chora

The Islands

Corfu

10km
5 miles

N

Corfu (Kerkyra)

Luxuriantly beautiful Corfu is a Garden of Eden cast up in the northwest corner of Greece, a sweet mockery of the grim grey mountains of Albania, so close and so unenticing. From Shakespeare to Edward Lear, from Gladstone to Lawrence and Gerald Durrell, Corfu has long held a special place in the English heart. Its reputation as a distant paradise began with Homer, who called it Scheria, the happy isle of the Phaeacians, beloved of the gods, where the shipwrecked Odysseus was entertained by the lovely Nausica. Shakespeare made it the magical isle of The Tempest, where Prospero offered a different sort of hospitality to his shipwrecked guests. The unique Venetian city-capital of the island is one of the loveliest and most elegant in Greece; if you squint, perhaps, you won't notice that nearly every building's ground floor has been given over to souvenir shops and tourist bars. For it's a sad and unavoidable fact that no other island (except Rhodes) has been so exploited and developed: every year Paradise descends a little closer to an international package tour Babylon for lager louts.

For all that, head into the hinterland (especially in the mountains to the north) and you'll find villages and landscapes blissfully virgin of monster concrete hotels, enclaves of expensive villas, tourist compounds and golf courses. Come in the off season (good times are early spring, when the almonds blossom, around Palm Sunday or the first part of November, coinciding with the colourful celebrations of Ag. Spyridon), and seek out the old cobbled donkey paths that in Venetian times provided the main link between villages, and you'll be rewarded with a poignant vision of the old Corfu, strewn with wild flowers, scented with the blossoms of lemons and kumquats, silvery with forests of ancient olives—which still outnumber tourists by three and half million. Just don't go out without your wet-weather clothes.

History

In ancient times Corfu was Corcyra, named after a mistress of the sea god Poseidon. She bore him a son called Phaeax, who became the founder of the Phaeacian race. In 734 BC the Corinthians sent a trading colony to the island and founded a city at Paliapolis; modern Analypsis was the site of the Corinthian citadel-acropolis.

Although Corcyra thrived to become the richest of the Ionian islands, it was cursed with violent political rivalries between its democrats and the oligarchs.

Although the Corcyrian fleet defeated the ships of Corinth when the two quarrelled over a colony in Albania (the dispute that set off the Peloponnesian war) internal strife had so weakened Corcyra that at the beginning of the 4th century BC it was captured first by Syracuse, and then by King Pyrrhus of Epirus and in 229 BC by the Illyrians. Yet whatever the turmoil, ancient Corcyra never lost its lofty reputation for fertility and beauty; Nero, the ham emperor, paid it a special visit in AD 67 to dance and sing at the temple of Zeus in modern Kassiopi.

The remnants of the population that survived the ravages of the Goths founded a new town on the two hills of Cape Sidaro where they would be better protected (*corypho* in Greek means two peaks, hence 'Corfu'). It failed to thwart the Normans in 1081, and in 1148 when their raids menaced the Byzantine Empire itself, Emperor Emmanuel Comnenus sent a special force and fleet to dislodge them. When the siege of the Byzantines made no progress, Emmanuel came to lead the attack in person. By craftily causing subversion among the Normans themselves, he succeeded in winning back the island.

In 1204, when Venice came to claim Corfu, the inhabitants put up a stiff resistance. Although the Venetians succeeded in taking the island's forts, the islanders aligned themselves with the Despotat of Epirus, an Orthodox state. Fifty years later, however, the King of Naples and brother of St Louis of France, Charles I of Anjou, snatched Corfu and the rest of Achaia when his son married the princess of Villehardouin. Angevin rule, already infamous for provoking the Sicilian Vespers, was equally intolerant and hateful on Corfu. After 120 years, the Corfiots swallowed their pride and in 1386 asked Venice to put them under the protection of the Republic.

In 1537 a serious threat, not only to Corfu but to all of Europe, landed at Igoumenitsa in the form of Suleiman the Magnificent. Suleiman, the greatest of the Turkish sultans, already had most of the rest of Greece under his belt and was determined to take Corfu as a base for attacking Italy and Western Europe. Thanks to a peace treaty with Venice, Suleiman was able to plot his attack in the utmost secrecy. When the Corfiots discovered only a few days in advance what was in store for them, they tore down their houses for stone to repair the fortress and to leave nothing behind for the Turks. The terrible Barbarossa was the first to arrive and begin the siege of the city, during which he suffered massive losses. Thousands of Corfiots who had been pitilessly abandoned outside the fortress were caught in the Venetian and Turkish crossfire, and fell prey to Barbarossa's fits of rage at his continual setbacks. Those who managed to survive were carted off to the slave markets of Constantinople when Suleiman, discouraged by his losses and bad weather, ordered the withdrawal of the siege.

Only 21 years later Venice, under pressure from the Corfiots, expanded the island's fortifications to include the town. Many houses were left unprotected, however, and when the Turks reappeared in 1571 under Ouloudj Ali, these and the rest of the villages, trees and vineyards on Corfu were decimated. This time the Turks took no prisoners and massacred whoever they caught. The devastation was given a final touch two years later by another pirate admiral, Sinan Pasha: of the entire Corfiot population, only a tenth remained on the island after 1573.

In 1576 Venice finally began to build the walls required for the safety of all the Corfiots, together with the Fortezza Nuova and other fortifications designed by the expert Sammicheli; few remains of these still exist but they were considered superb in their day. They were given the ultimate test in 1716, when Turks staged furious attacks for one terrible month, before being repulsed by a tempest sent by Ag. Spyridon, Corfu's patron saint.

After the fall of Venice, the French occupied Corfu but quickly lost it again in a fierce battle against the Russo–Turkish fleet. When Napoleon finally got the island back, he personally designed new fortifications for the town. These were so formidable that the British, when allotted the Ionian islands after Waterloo, did not care to attack them when the French commander Donzelot refused to give them up. The French government finally had to order Donzelot home, and in 1815 Corfu came under British protection with the blessing of Count John Capodistria. Capodistria, soon to be the first president of Greece, was a native of Corfu and at that time was working for the Tsar of Russia.

But while Capodistria had requested 'military protection', the British, based in Corfu, took upon themselves all the affairs of the Ionian State. One of the first things they did was demolish part of the Venetian walls to build new, more powerful ones in their place, calling upon the Ionian government to cough up more than a million gold sovereigns to pay for the improvements. But in 1864, when the Brits decided to pull out and let the Ionian islands unite with Greece, it was with the ungracious condition that they first destroy the fortresses of Corfu—not only the walls they themselves had just made the Corfiots build but also the historic Venetian buildings. A wave of protest from all corners of the Greek world failed to move the British, and in 1864 the fortifications were blown up, leaving substantial remains standing today. In 1923 Mussolini bombarded and occupied Corfu after the assassination on Greek territory of an Italian delegate to the Greek–Albanian border council; the Italians left only when Greece paid a large indemnity. An even worse bombardment occurred in 1943, when the Germans blasted the city and its Italian garrison for ten days; a year later, the British and Americans bombed the Germans. At the end of the war, a quarter of the old city was destroyed, including 14 of the loveliest churches.

Connections

By air: Frequent charter flights from London, Manchester and Glasgow; also regular flights from many European cities; three flights a day from Athens, two in the winter. The Olympic Airways office in Corfu town is at Kapodistriou 20, © (0661) 38 694/5/6. There is no special bus service linking Corfu's airport to the town, but there is a regular bus stop on the main road, several hundred metres away.

By sea: Year-round ferries from Brindisi, Bari and Ancona (ships stop en route to Patras, most allowing a free stop-over in Corfu. You must specify this when you purchase your ticket). A catamaran links Brindisi to Corfu in 3½ hours (Corfu: Charitos Travel, 35 Arseniou, © (0661) 44 611; Athens: 28 Nikis Syntagma, © (01) 322 0503). Services to Croatia are suspended. Also in the summer ferries sail from Igoumenitsa, less frequently off season. In season there are connections with Patras, Ithaca, Kefalonia and a year round daily ferry to Paxos, including links with the small islands of Ereikoussa, Othoni and Mathraki. Frequent buses run from Athens and Thessaloniki to Igoumenitsa.

By bus: The central bus depot in Plateia Theotoki–San Rocco Square has blue buses to villages just beyond the city (Potamos, Gouvia, Dassia, Benitses). The depot in Avramiou St has connections, green buses, to the more distant villages (Glyfada, Paliokastritsa, Ag. Stefanos, Roda), as well as to Athens (leaving at 9am, journey time 11 hours) and Thessaloniki.

Tours: Travel agents in Corfu offer one-day classical tours to the mainland: to Epirus to visit the Oracle of the Dead (consulted by Odysseus after crossing the perilous River Styx), and the ancient cities of Kassopea and Nicopolis, founded by Augustus after the defeat of Mark Anthony and Cleopatra in 31 BC. A second tour takes in Dodoni, with its ancient theatre and Ioannina, the modern capital of Epirus, with its island of Ali Pasha and museum.

Tourist Information

EOT, New Fortress Square (behind the new fort in the old port), © (0661) 37 520/638.

Tourist police, in the old port behind the Palace of St Michael and St George, © 30 265.

Consulates

Great Britain	2 SS Alexandras, © 30 055 and 37 995
Germany	57 Guilford St, © 31 755
France	15 Desillas St, © 30 067

Corfu Town

Corfu town, or Kerkyra, the largest town in the Ionian islands, was laid out by the Venetians in the 14th century, when the medieval town, crowded onto the peninsula of Cape Sidaro (where the old fortress now stands) had no room to expand. They began with the quarter known as Campiello, where narrow three- or four-storey houses loom over the narrow streets, as they do back in the lagoon capital. By the time the new walls were added in the 16th century, the Venetians built at a more leisurely pace in the more open style of the Renaissance, laying out an exquisite series of central streets and small squares. The British knocked down a number of old Venetian walls to allow for further growth, and then built a set of elegant Georgian public buildings.

Besides Campiello, the old city is divided into a number of small quarters. The 19th-century residential district to the south is called Garitsa; if you arrive from Italy, you enter the city through its back door at Mandouki or New Port, west of the New Fortress. Mandouki isn't one of the more attractive parts of town, but it's a good place to look for cheap rooms and food. The ferries from the mainland and islands call to the east of the New Port, at the Old Port.

The New Fortress

Confusingly, the Old Port is dominated by the New Fortress, or Neo Frourio, where many people get their first look at the town; this was built by the Venetians following the third attack on Corfu, although most of the walls were destroyed by the British. The New Fortress bore the brunt of the Turks' siege of 1716. Once a Greek naval base, it is now open to the public. It offers excellent views of Corfu Town and boasts two underground tunnels. Corfu Market is situated in the Fortress's moat in Markora Street. Get there early to get the pick of the fresh fish and produce on sale. One street near the fortress is named for the crafty and heroic Marshal Schulenburg, a soldier of fortune from Saxony, who outwitted the Turkish High Admiral in the Great Siege—the last major attempt of the Ottoman Empire to expand in the west. Near the green bus station stands the 1749 Catholic Church of Tenedos, named after an icon brought to Corfu by the Venetians from the Turkish island of Tenedos.

From the Old Port you can reach the centre of town through the 16th-century Spilia Gate, incorporated into a later structure, or take the narrow steps next to the Hotel Nea Yorki into the medieval Campiello Quarter (*see* below); the Jewish Quarter, equally old and picturesque, lies at the south end of the fortress walls. Although the synagogue remains in the heart of the quarter, few of its congregation survived the concentration camps to return to Corfu.

The Esplanade

A series of long parallel streets—the main residential district of the Venetians—all lead to the town's centre, the great green space called the Spinada or **Esplanade**, one of the largest public squares in Europe. Originally the area was left open for defensive purposes; under Napoleon it began to take its present form as a garden and promenade. The French arcades of the Liston on the west edge are full of cafés, the flowerbeds are immaculately kept, and at night the monuments and trees are floodlit for dramatic effect.

The northern end of the Esplanade is occupied by the Georgian **Palace of St Michael and St George** with its two grand gates. Designed by Sir George Whitmore, the palace was built as the residence of Sir Thomas Maitland, first High Commissioner of the Ionian islands—hence the symbols of the seven islands that adorn the façade. In 1864 it became the residence of the King of Greece, then fell into disuse until it was renovated in 1953 to house a **Museum of Far Eastern Art**, one of the largest single-owned collections in the world, and the only one of its kind in Greece. The impressive collection, a gift to Corfu from two diplomats,

Gregory Manos and Micholos Chadjivasiliou, contains 10,000 works from all the countries of the Far East dating back to 1000 BC. The palace also houses the public library. Note that during 1994, the museum will be in storage to provide space in the palace for European cultural exhibitions.

Just in front of the palace is another oddity left over from British rule—the **cricket ground**, where little boys play football until their older white-clad brothers chase them off the field. In the summer, matches are held, pitting the six local teams against visitors from Britain, the Greek mainland and Europe.

Numerous monuments embellish the Esplanade. Towards the centre is the **memorial to Sir Thomas Maitland**, another work of Sir George Whitmore, designed in the form of an Ionian rotunda. Near here is the British-built bandstand, where the local brass bands, an *opera buffo* speciality of Corfu (you can often hear them practising in the evening in the old quarters) perform in the summer. There is a heroic marble **statue of Marshal Schulenburg**, and most charmingly, a seated statue of Corfu's favourite Englishman, the Hellenophile Frederick North, Earl of Guilford (better known as Lord North) (1769–1828), who with Capodistria founded the first university in Greece. The **Guilford Memorial** portrays him in ancient robes, a touch which he would probably have appreciated. A statue of his friend, Count Capodistria, first president of Greece, stands towards the southern end of the Esplanade.

The **Old Fortress** on Cape Sidaro is separated from the Esplanade by the moat, or contra fosse, dug over a 100-year period by the Venetians. The medieval town of Corfu was located on the two little hills of the cape; scholars have identified the site with the Heraion acropolis mentioned by Thucydides. The fortress' walls, built up over the centuries, were badly damaged by the Brits; others have fallen into decay. Part of the fortress is still used by the Greek army, but you can wander about and explore the Venetian tunnels, battlements, drawbridge, the Venetian well, cannons dating back to 1684 and **St George's**, the church of the British garrison. Best of all, however, is the view of the city from the hills. In the summer there's a **Sound and Light Show**, and evening performances of **folkdancing** (*1 June–30 Sept; combined ticket 600 dr.*).

Ag. Spyridon

The church of Corfu's patron saint Ag. Spyridon is in the old town, not far from the Ionian and Popular Bank of Greece. It's easy to find: the campanile soars above town like the mast of a ship, covered with flags and Christmas lights. Ag. Spyridon was the Bishop of Cyprus in the 4th century; when Constantinople fell to the Turks, his bones were smuggled in a sack of straw to Corfu. The church was built in 1596 to house the precious relics, no longer in straw but contained in a silver Renaissance reliquary which with great pomp is carted though town on the saint's feast days. According to the Corfiots, the good saint has brought them safely through many trials, frightening both cholera and the Turks away from his beloved worshippers. He even gave the Catholics a good scare when they considered placing an altar in his church; the night before its dedication, he blew up a powder magazine in the Old Fortress with a bolt of lightning to show his displeasure. The Orthodox Palm Sunday, Easter Saturday, 11 August and the first Sunday in November are dedicated to huge celebrations for Ag. Spyridon.

The nearby Ionian Bank houses a **Museum of Paper Money**, with a collection of banknotes from around the world, and Greek notes dating from the nation's birth. The second floor is given over to an exhibition demonstrating the various stages in the production of banknotes. Across the square, the 1689 church of the **Holy Virgin Faneromeni** contains some fine icons of the Ionian School.

The square gives on to the main street **Nikiforou Theotoki**, one of the prettiest in the town. From there head up E. Voulgareos St to the elegant square with Corfu's **Town Hall**, a lovely Venetian confection begun in 1691 that later did duty as the municipal opera house. The **Catholic Cathedral of St James** on the square was seriously damaged by the German bombing in 1943; only the bell tower survived intact. The rest has been reconstructed.

Campiello

There are a number of buildings worth seeking out in the Campiello quarter between the Old Port and the Esplanade, beginning with the 1577 **Orthodox Cathedral**, dedicated to Ag. Theodora Augusta, Empress of Byzantium and canonized for her role in restoring icon worship in the Orthodox Church following the Iconoclasm. Her relics were brought to Corfu along with those of Ag. Spyridon. The cathedral façade dates from the 18th century and the interior is richly adorned with 16th- to 18th-century icons. The **Byzantine Museum of Corfu** is near here, up the steps from Arseniou St, with fine exhibits of Byzantine icons (at time of writing closed indefinitely for restoration). On the same street is the **Solomos Museum**, with a collection of old photographs and memorabilia associated with the poet Dionysos Solomos (*open 8.45–3, Tues-Sat, 9.30-2.30, Sun; closed Mon*).

On a narrow stairway off Philharmoniki St, **Ag. Nikolaos** had the distinction of once serving as the parish church for the King of Serbia. After the defeat of the Serbian army by the Austro–Hungarians in 1916, the King, his government, and some 150,000 Serbs took refuge on Corfu. A third of them died shortly thereafter from the flu and are buried on **Vido island**. Boats from the Old Port regularly make the trip to Vido; the Venetians fortified it after the Turks built a gun battery on it to attack the Old Fortress in 1537. The walls were demolished by the British. Today the island is a quiet refuge with footpaths, a little beach, and a memorial to the Serbs. It is also home to the Kerkyra Bird and Wildlife Sanctuary, set up to treat birds often injured during the shooting season. There is also an impressive collection of exotic birds from cockatoos to macaws.

Garitsa and the Southern Suburbs

South of the Old Fortress, **Garitsa Bay** is believed to have been the harbour of King Alcinoos of the Phaeacians. Amid its neo-Classical buildings, is a **Municipal Art Gallery** on Moustoxidi St (*Open 10–1 and 6–9*), and on Kolokotroni St the **British Cemetery** is set in beautiful, peaceful gardens; the graves, many with intriguing headstones, date from the beginning of British protectorate.

The star attraction in the district of Garitsa is the **Archaeology Museum** (*open 8.30–3, Sun 9.30–2.30, closed Mon*), with an excellent collection of finds from the island and nearby mainland, including the famous wall-sized Gorgon Pediment discovered near the 5th-century BC temple of Artemis Kanoni, housed in a room all to itself. Other items are from the 7th-century BC **Menecrates tomb**, found in the 19th century in an excellent state of preservation, and still standing at the junction of Marassli and Kiprou St.

South of Garitsa is the suburb of **Anemomilos** ('windmills'), where for a small fee you can swim at the beach of **Mon Repos**. Mon Repos palace above was built by Sir Frederick, the second High Commissioner of the Ionian State, for his Corfiot wife. The Greek royal family later adopted it as a summer villa; the Duke of Edinburgh, Phil the Greek, was born there. Here, too, is one of the oldest churches on the island, the 11th-century **Ag. Iassonos and Sosipater** (two martyrs instructed by St Paul). Recent excavations have uncovered what is thought to be the Temple of Apollo, dating from the 15th-century BC. The martyrs' tombs and rare icons are inside; the church is one of the island's best examples of Byzantine architecture.

It is a short stroll to **Analypsis**, just south of Mon Repos. Near the Venetian church, along the wall of Mon Repos, a path leads to the **spring of Kardaki**, which flows from the mouth of a lion; the Venetians used it to supply their ships. The cold water is good, but an inscription above warns: 'Every stranger who wets his lips here to his home will not return.' Below the spring are the ruins of a 6th-century BC temple. It is one of the most tranquil spots in Corfu.

Kanoni, at the southern tip of the little peninsula, is named for the old cannon once situated on the bluff, where two cafés now overlook the pretty bay, the harbour of ancient Corcyra. Two islets protected it: that of the picturesque convent **Panayia Vlancharina**, now connected to the shore by a causeway, and **Pontikonisi**, the Isle of the Mouse, with a 13th-century chapel, **Ag. Pnevmatos**. Pontikonisi was the Phoenician ship that brought Odysseus home to Ithaca, but which, on its way home, the angry Poseidon smote 'with his open palm, and made the ship a rock, fast rooted in the bed of the deep sea', according to the *Odyssey*. Bus no. 3 from Corfu town passes all the above suburbs of gardens and trees, its route ending at Kanoni. It's worth noting that Kanoni overlooks Corfu's airport, and the noise of planes day and night can interrupt a good night's sleep, in case you were thinking of staying in Kanoni.

(*0661–*)   ***Where to Stay***

luxury

There's a cache of luxurious high rise palaces in Kanoni, like the **Corfu Hilton**, a hotel and bungalow complex, ✆ 36 540, fax 36551and one of the few hotels in Greece with a bowling alley, but a room here could cost 30,000 dr. in high season. In the same league, north of Corfu town, at Komeno Bay, is the **Astir Palace**, ✆ 91 481, fax 91881.

expensive

For old-style elegance, no hotel on Corfu can compete with the **Cavalieri Corfu**, located on the Esplanade at 4 Kapodistriou, ✆ 39 336, in a renovated French mansion; comfortable, air conditioned and rated class A. In the old port there's the **Astron Hotel** in a charming neo-Classical structure at 15 Donzelotou, ✆ 39 505.

moderate

The **Bella Venezia**, 4 Napoleon Zambeli, is a renovated old building in a quiet part of the centre of town, ✆ (0661) 46 500. If you'd prefer something newer, there's always the **Europa** at the New Port (Mandouki, ✆ 39 304) which has, along with modern, clean rooms, and a self-service laundrette. A little further along the Esplanade from the Cavalieri Hotel is a class C hotel, the **Arcadion** at 44 Kapodistriou, ✆ 37 671. Next to it, in another old building, is the gallant class D **Hotel New York**, ✆ 39 922. Much lower on the price scale to the competition in Kanoni, but in an equally commanding position is the **Royal**, a C class hotel that could be luxury class, with its three swimming pools on descending levels, roof garden and its fine view over Mouse Island and the airport's busy runway, © 37 512.

cheap

For something less dear, you could go to the **National Tourist Office**, © 37 520/638, and pick up their list of rooms to let in town. Most of these are in the old quarters and cost 4000 dr. upwards for a bed in season.

Eating Out

At some point of your stay in Corfu you'll spend some time relaxing on the Esplanade, at the Liston, watching the crowds go by or cheering on the local cricket team. Eating in that area can be expensive, but one place that serves good, authentic Greek dishes at a reasonable price is the **Acteon**. One street back on Kapodistriou, **Rex** is even better value—try the local speciality *sofrito* (meat stew with garlic) and pay 2000 dr. for a meal. Just as good is **Dionysos**, off N. Theotiki. The **Bella Napoli** serves international cuisine, with a bias on Italian (3000–4000 dr.). In Kremasti Square the **Venetian Well** has a varied menu which changes daily: Greek, international and oriental specialities (2500 dr.). **Pizza Pete**, in Arseniou St, overlooking the old port, prides himself on the best in town—a pizza meal will run to 1000 dr. Down in Mandouki, where the ferries dock, **Xenichtes**, 12 Potamou, serves excellent Greek food with a sprinkling of dishes from other countries (2500 dr.), and the **Averof**, at Alipou and Prosselendou St, is a long-established favourite of tourists and locals alike. In Xen. Stratigou St, the smart **Orestes** has dining inside and in a pleasant little garden opposite; if you order their seafood specialities, you'll pay 3000 dr. There are several other fish restaurants in the same area.

South of the fortress in Garitsa one of the most popular and reliable tavernas is **Koromios**, where it's difficult to run up a bill of more than 2500 dr. A little way out of town to the south at Kinopiastes is **Tripa**, where you can watch folkdancing from your table. Greek nights here are renowned, with up to 10 courses served; although it's not cheap, the food and service are excellent. Nearby, on the Achillion road (about 7km from town) are two tavernas with live music and good, reasonably priced food, the **Barbathomas**, with meat specialities, and **Pontis**, with a big selection of mezedes, spit-roasted lamb, charcoal grills and local dishes; you can eat well at either for 2500 dr. On the road out to Kontokali (take a taxi) the **Mandarin Palace Chinese Restaurant** has an excellent reputation for top class food and swift service, and its splendid view does justice to the Peking Duck (3000 dr.). For a perfectly artificial evening, **Danilia's Village** is a reconstruction of a typical, old Corfiot settlement, with museum, shopping arcade, folklore museum, and displays of traditional Ionian dancing. It's one of Corfu's bigger attractions and a colourful night out, although the food doesn't match the quality of the floor show. Tickets available from most travel agents or you hotel reception.

North of Corfu Town

The roads along the east coast of Corfu are quite good and hotel and resort developers have followed them nearly every inch of the way. To the immediate north begins a long series of beach, hotel and restaurant complexes, along with most of Corfu's campsites, at Kontokali, Gouvia, Dassia, Ipsos and Pirgi. **Kontokali**, 8km from Corfu town, and **Gouvia**, a little further north, overlook a lagoon once used by the Venetians as a harbour, and today as a popular marina for visiting yachts. Both villages offer watersports and reasonable swimming off the pebble beach. A few kilometres further north **Dassia** has a long, narrow sand and shingle beach fringed by olive groves, a favourite for sports from waterskiing to paragliding. From here you can take boat trips to Kassiopi (north), Mouse Island and Benitses (south).

If a good night's sleep is a priority, avoid **Ipsos**, north of Dassia, where the plethora of bars and discos reverberate till dawn. Its long scimitar of beach set against cliffs in the background is attractive. Again, there are plenty of watersports along this stretch of sand which extends into the small village of **Pirgi**, now totally given over to tourism. You can escape the frenetic crowds by carrying on just to the north, where the mountains meet the sea to form a series of small coves and tiny beaches. Here, **Kouloura**, a kilometre or so from the rugged Albanian coast, is a lovely seaside hamlet, which (as yet) has not succumbed to the developers, unlike its neighbour **Kalami**. Kouloura was favoured by Venetians: note the 16th-century **Kouartanou Gennata**, part villa and part fortified tower, and two 17th-century mansions, **Vassila** and **Prosalenti**. Near Kouloura, a steep, twisting path descends to the pretty **Kaminaki** beach; the reward is a fine pebbly beach with the clearest of water. There are some water sports here, and a few beach tavernas. The brothers Durrell lived in a seaside villa here in the 1930s. Both have written about the island: Lawrence Durrell in *Prospero's Cell* and Gerald, the naturalist, in *My Family and Other Animals*.

Between Kouloura and Ag. Stefanos is the picturesque and unspoilt bay of **Agni**. Until recently it was only accessible by boat, but now a road has been built to the beach, where there are three excellent tavernas which are also cheap. The crystal clear waters of Agni have made it a favourite swimming spot.

Behind Kouloura looms 900m **Mt Pantokrator**, Corfu's highest point. Its slopes can be tackled from the village of **Nissaki** (south), a charming fishing hamlet and quiet resort, where goat tracks lead down to little coves. From Nissaki, find your way to the village of **Palio Sinies**, from where the path to the summit of Pantokrator is an arduous one, but rewarded with a wondrous display of flora, and a view of emerald Corfu spread at your feet and white-capped Albanian peaks on the mainland.

Kassiopi

Kassiopi lies at the northern end of the good paved road. An important Hellenistic town founded by Pyrrhus of Epirus, Kassiopi flourished under the Romans who surrounded it with great walls. Its famous shrine of Zeus Cassius was visited by Cicero and Emperor Nero; its Byzantine fortress was the first place in Greece to fall to Robert Guiscard's Normans, who invaded from their fief in Calabria, after first pillaging Rome. As every subsequent marauder from the north passed by Kassiopi to reach Corfu town, the town bore the brunt of their attacks. When after a long struggle the Venetians finally took the fortress, they rendered it useless to avenge themselves. Without their defences the Kassiopians suffered terribly at the hands of the Turks and the town lost all of its former importance.

The ruined fortress still stands above the village, guarding only wild flowers and sheep. Although still a fishing village, Kassiopi has discovered the profits to be made from the tourist trade and has become one of Corfu's busiest resorts, with a more refined atmosphere than Benitses. Most visitors stay in smart apartments or villas; there are no hotels. There are four small, well-equipped beaches reached by footpath from the headland, and when you're tired of windsurfing or basting yourself on the beach you can explore the rocky coastline on foot. The more hardy can go inland towards **Bodholahos**, where a fairly steep climb into the hinterland affords beautiful views of Kassiopi and coastline.

If you take the road from **Spartilas** to **Perithia**, a charming cobblestoned village nestling in the hills, you'll have a rough but memorable ride through some of the island's most beautiful countryside. **Ag. Panteleimonos**, another inland village, has a huge ruined tower mansion called **Polylas**, complete with prisons used during the Venetian occupation. All along the north coast from **Roda** (another small resort, where egg and chips seems to be everyone's special of the day) to Sidari are fine sandy beaches, considered among the best on Corfu; one is **Acharavi**, a half-hour walk east from Roda, with a large sand and shingle beach framed by gorgeous scenery.

Sidari, although almost entirely given over to tourism (like so many Corfu resorts, British tour operators seem to have the monopoly), is one of the most charming spots on the island, a contrast of lush greenery and picturesque sandstone cliffs, eroded by the wind to form strangely shaped caves. In the bay is the **Canal d'Amour**, a peculiar rock formation said to be two lovers—swim between them and you are guaranteed eternal love, which is more than can be said for the local disco. There are less crowded beaches near Sidari at **Peroulades**, whose sandy beach is divided by a cliff; at **Arillas**, a wide, sandy bay with an attractive back-drop of green hills; at **Ag. Stefanos**, a rather characterless bay with villas and served by two hotels, yet nonetheless uncrowded even at the height of summer; and at **Ag. Georgios**, another long, sandy stretch of beach under steep cliffs, just in the budding stages of development. This whole northwest corner of Corfu is covered with forests. The main roads have been resurfaced, but once off the beaten track be warned that the roads can bottom out the best shock absorbers. Between Sidari and Roda, **Karoussades**, with the 16th-century mansion of the Theotoki family, is a pretty agricultural centre; there is good swimming at sandy **Astrakeri** beach.

Northwest of Corfu are three islets, **Othonos** (the largest), **Erikoussa** and **Mathraki**, comprising the westernmost territory of Greece. The easiest way to visit the islands is on an organized excursion from Sidari or Corfu, or in the summer from Ag. Stefanos. On Othonos a well-preserved medieval fort, **Kastri**, can be seen on a pine-covered hill. Olives and grapes are produced locally, and fresh fish is always available. Many places on the islets are still without electricity, and the population consists mainly of women whose husbands fish or otherwise work in the USA.

Paliokastritsa, endowed with a beautiful horseshoe bay and sandy coves, olive and almond groves, mountains and forests, has become the major resort area in west Corfu, jam-packed in the summer with holiday-makers and day-trippers; in the early spring, however, you can easily believe its claim to have been the fabled home of the princess Nausica. On a promontory above town, **Paliokastritsa monastery** was built in 1228 on the site of a Byzantine fortress, and tarted up by an abbot with rococo taste in the 1700s. Inside, a one-room museum contains some very old icons; outside, a peach of a view of the sapphire sea below. The best view of all however, is on the steep climb (or drive) out of Paliokastritsa through cypress and pine woods towards the village of **Lakones** and its celebrated Bella Vista taverna. Behind Lakones rises the island's third highest peak, with more splendid views over the island.

Lakones itself is the hub of the loveliest walks on Corfu, especially to the formidable **Angelokastro** (you can also walk from Paliokastritsa). Built in the 13th century by the Byzantine despot of Epirus, Michael Angelos, it is mostly ruined, but makes an impressive sight perched on the wild red rocks over a 300m precipice. Angelokastro played a major role during the various raids on the island, sheltering the surrounding villagers (as well as the Venetian governor, who lived there). However, the Corfiots were rarely content to stay behind the walls of Angelokastro, and often spilled out to attack their attackers. If you have a car, the mountain roads from Lakones north to Roda through the little villages of **Choreopiskopi**, **Valanion** (3km on a byroad) and **Nimfes** offer a lovely bucolic journey through the Corfu of yesteryear.

East of Paliokastritsa stretches the fertile, startlingly flat and intensely cultivated **Ropa plain**. To the south are good beaches and resorts at **Ermones** (another candidate for Odysseus' landing point) and **Glyfada**, one of the island's best. Unfortunately it fills up during the day with hotel residents and day-trippers, but early evening is perfect for a swim here, with steep cliffs dropping straight down into the blue bay. **Pelekas**, a 17th-century village up on a mountain ridge, was Kaiser Wilhelm II's favourite spot to watch the sunset; busloads of people come out every evening in the summer to do the same, from a tower known as the **Kaiser's Throne**. During the day, Miriotissa beach at Pelekas is Corfu's unofficial naturist beach. After sunset the village throbs to the sound of disco music.

The half of the island south of Corfu town has attracted the worst excesses of tourism on the island, especially the east coast. The more inaccessible west coast is more worthwhile: continuing south of Pelekas is **Ag. Gordios** with a lovely, sheltered 2-mile-long beach that so far has scarcely been developed. A Byzantine castle at **Gardiki**, south of Ag. Gordios, was another work by the despot of Epirus, Michael Angelos II. This is one of the most unspoilt areas of Corfu, and is a good starting point for some excellent walks. A minor road by Gardiki leads in 4km to Corfu's only lake, **Limni Korission**, which is separated from the sea by a long stretch of dunes; in spring and autumn it fills with migratory birds. Nearby **Ag. Mathias** is a serene place to daydream under the plane tree and write up your diary, disturbed only by the occasional roar of hired scooters and jeeps as they zip through the village on a quest for true peace and quiet in this least discovered corner of the island. The village remains delightfully Greek, where the locals are more concerned about their olive crop than threatened decreases in tourist numbers. There are 24 churches in, or near, the village, and by asking around you can find your way down the steep hill slopes to the really peaceful beaches of **Tria Avlakia, Paramonas** and **Skithi**, with a few rooms and the odd inexpensive taverna. **Lagoudia**, two islets off the southwest coast, are the home of a tribe of donkeys; some of their ancestors were eaten by a boatload of Frenchmen who were wrecked there for three days.

Other fine beaches, deserted for the most part, line the southwest coast to **Ag. Georgios**, recommended for its swimming, although the village has few charms. **Lefkimi**, in the centre of a large fertile plain, is Corfu's second most important village but not terribly interesting if you aren't a farmer; nearby **Kavos**, once an important fishing village, has become the lager lout haven of Corfu with wall-to-wall bars and neon lights. It's best avoided unless you want to dance the night away. **Prokopios** at Arkodila has an excellent beach with all variety of watersports; it also has a limited but lively nightlife as does **Asprocavos**, both famous for their white sand.

Heading north up the east coast towards Corfu town, **Moraitika, Miramare** and **Benitses** are tourist babylons. British pubs and rowdy crowds have turned Benitses into Corfu's Costa Brava (at its worst), to the point where many of the resort's former enthusiasts have moved out of earshot. One family diversion in Benitses is the **shell museum**, with a colourful collection of shells, coral, fossils, starfish and other natural treasure from the sea (*daily 10–7*). To escape Benitses on foot, walk through the old, residential quarter of the village, past the local cemetery and head off towards **Stavros** and the Benitses Waterworks, built by Sir Frederick Adam, British High Commissioner from 1824–32, a walk through some delightful rural scenery.

For something completely different, visit Corfu's casino (*summer only*) and museum in the Italianate **Achilleion** near Gastouri, perhaps the best kitsch palace in all of Greece—used as a location for the James Bond film *For Your Eyes Only*. Built in 1890 by the Empress Elisabeth ('Sissi') of Austria, the villa was named for that lady's passion for the hero of Homer's *Iliad*; a large marble statue of the wounded Achilles stands in the garden. When Sissi was assassinated in 1898 by an Italian anarchist, Kaiser Wilhelm made the Achilleion his summer residence from 1908 to 1914. The small museum (*8.45–3.30*) contains, among its curious collection of imperial mementoes, the Kaiser's riding saddle, from which he dictated some of his plans for the First World War. **Perama** on the coast, claims to be the site of King Alcinoos' wonderful garden, and still offers more luxury and swish villas to rent than any other place on this luxurious island.

Festivals

10 July, Ag. Prokopios at Kavos; 14 August, The Procession of Lights at Mandouki; first Friday after Easter, Paliokastritsa; 5–8 July, at Lefkimi; 15 August, Panayias at Kassiopi; 21 May, Union with Greece; procession of Ag. Spyridon in Corfu town on Palm Sunday, Easter, 11 August and first Sunday in November.

(*0663–*)   ### Where to Stay

expensive

In lovely Paliokastritsa everything is overpriced; the **Akrotiri Beach**, five minutes uphill from the beach enjoys some of the best views, and there's a swimming pool for those who don't want to commute to the sea, ✆ 41 275. If you're lucky (or book early) you may get one of the eight rooms right on the beach at the **Pavillion Xenia**, ✆ 41 208, with a good restaurant below, and priceless view and location. Glyfada beach is dominated by the **Grand Glyfada Hotel** and its many watersport activities, ✆ (0661) 94 201, fax 30184. The **Three Brothers** hotel in Sidari may be full of package tourists, but if they haven't got a room they'll know where to find one, ✆ 95 342. Lastly, for dramatic modern architecture on the beach, stay at the **Ag. Gordios** on Ag. Gordios, © 96 213. Renting villas is big usiness on Corfu: pick up details from any travel agency.

moderate

There are plenty of hotels in the moderate price range on the coast north of Corfu town, such as the **Pyrros**, © 91 206, at Kontokali, the **Galaxias** at Gouvia, © 91 223, and the **Doria** at Dassia, © 93 865, all at around 6000–8000 dr. for a room, although it's wise to book or at least ring ahead. Some very presentable D class hotels are the **Costas Beach**, © 93 205, at Ipsos, or the **Louvre** at Gouvia, © 91 508, but don't expect any original masterpieces here.

cheap

For rooms and information on accommodation outside Corfu town, contact the Tourist Police near the waterfront on 43 Arseniou St, or at the Old Port, or one of the many tourist agencies. There's a **campground** 2km inland from Paliokastritsa; others are at Messoghi, Kontokali (the nearest to Corfu town), Ipsos, Karoussades (these two the best on the island), Pirgi and Dafnila. Nearly every village has rooms to let, some, like Kassiopi, Pelekas and Kavos, with long listings. Corfu's **youth hostel** is in Kontokali (take bus no. 7 from San Rocco Square, © 91 202), and an IYHF card is required.

Eating Out

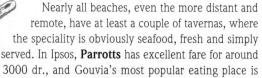

Nearly all beaches, even the more distant and remote, have at least a couple of tavernas, where the speciality is obviously seafood, fresh and simply served. In Ipsos, **Parrotts** has excellent fare for around 3000 dr., and Gouvia's most popular eating place is **Taverna Filippas** (2500 dr.). Up in Sidari the biggest culinary draw for many is the full works British breakfast, but good Greek food can be found at **Sophocles** and the **Canal D'Amour** for a fair price. Paliokastritsa has a number of seafood restaurants. **Chez George** commands the prime location and the highest prices; residents and long term visitors prefer the **Astakos** for its authentic food and reasonable prices. Drinking rather than eating seems to be the order of the day down in Benitses, but the **Marabou** bravely presents some tasty local dishes (2500 dr.), while **Pat's**

Place pulls in the visitors with good British standards like roast beef and two veg—2000 dr.

Ithaca (Ithaki)

Every traveller is a citizen of Ithaca.

—the sign in the port

Ithaca is one of those places that has become a compelling and universal symbol although many who have heard of it have no idea where it is, and those who do visit it usually have a hard time reconciling the island's reality with their idea of Odysseus' beloved home. And yet re-read your Homer before you come, and you'll find that nearly all of his descriptions of Ithaca fit this small mountainous island—it is indeed 'narrow' and 'rocky' and 'unfit for riding horses'. Some ancient and modern scholars, most famously the archaeologist Dörpfeld, have theorized that Homer's Ithaca was elsewhere—Lefkas and Kefalonia are popular contenders. Don't believe them. Ithaki as the locals call their home, the eternal symbol of all homes and journey's end, is the real thing, and 'even if you find it poor,' as Cavafy wrote, 'Ithaca does not deceive. Without Ithaca your journey would have no beauty'.

Ithaca has a jagged, indented coast (as Homer says), but no exceptional beaches and its roads are in such a state that most islanders prefer to travel to distant villages by caique. Its excellent harbour makes it a big favourite with sailors and best of all, it has changed little over the years. The atmosphere is relaxed and low-key, quiet and pleasant.

History

Inhabited from 2000 BC, Ithaca, the name of the prosperous Mycenaean kingdom of the intrepid Odysseus, is believed to have included not only the island proper but the four cities of Kefalonia. In the last 200 years scholars and archaeologists have sought for signs of Odysseus. Schliemann came after his great discovery of Troy, and since Schliemann inevitably found what he was looking for, he unearthed a large structure he immediately called 'Odysseus' Palace', and although it dates from a far later date (700 BC), the name has stuck. Later finds indicate that at least the ancients considered Ithaca Homer's Ithaca. Inscriptions indicate that Odysseus was worshipped as a divine hero, ancient coins bore Odysseus' picture, and pottery decorated with the cock, the symbol of Odysseus, has been found on the island. Homer describes the palace of Odysseus as above

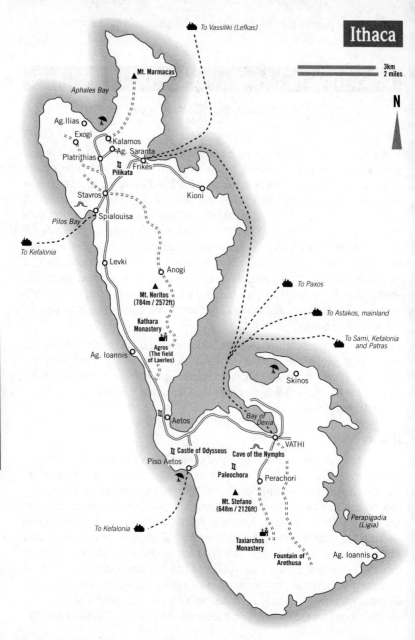

Ithaca

3km
2 miles

N

To Vassiliki (Lefkas)

Mt. Marmacas

Aphales Bay

Ag.Ilias
Exogi
Kalamos
Ag. Saranta
Platrithias
Frikes
Pilikata
Stavros
Kioni
Spialouisa
Pilos Bay

To Kefalonia

Levki
Anogi

Mt. Neritos
(784m / 2572ft)

Kathara
Monastery

Agros
(The field
of Laerles)

Ag. Ioannis

To Paxos

To Astakos, mainland

To Sami, Kefalonia
and Patras

Skinos

Aetos

Bay of
Dexia

VATHI

Castle of Odysseus

Piso Aetos

Cave of the Nymphs

Paleochora

Perachori

Perapigadia
(Ligia)

Mt. Stefano
(648m / 2126ft)

To Kefalonia

Taxiarchos
Monastery

Fountain of
Arethusa

Ag. Ioannis

'three seas' and in Stavros a hillock matches the description (over three bays) and is where in 1930 two ancient fortifications were discovered that may have been used for signals and beacons to the palace. Then there's the Fountain of Arethusa, where Odysseus met his faithful swineherd Eumaeus, and the cave where he hid the treasure given him by the Phaeacians.

After the Mycenaeans, Ithaca lost most of its importance and even its name; for a period it was humiliatingly known as 'Little Kefalonia'. By the time of the Venetians, invaders and pirates had so despoiled the island that it was all but abandoned, and the Venetians offered generous incentives to anyone who would settle and farm there. Once again Ithaca prospered, but unlike the other Ionian islands, it never had an aristocracy. Ironically, union with Greece in 1864 initiated the great migration from the island, many Ithakians going to Romania, Australia and South Africa. Like their countryman Odysseus, the islanders are well known as great sailors; even those who call Ithaca home spend much of the year away at sea.

Connections

Daily ferry with Patras, Kefalonia (Sami, Fiskardo and Ag. Efthimia), Vassiliki (Lefkas) and Astakos; frequent connections to Corfu, Paxos and Igoumenitsa.

Tourist Police

See regular police at Vathi, ℗ (0674) 32 205.

Vathi and the South

Vathi, built around the end of a long sheltered bay, is the capital of the island, although little larger than a village itself. Its beautiful harbour, surrounded by mountains on all sides, holds a wooded islet called **Lazaretto** in its embrace, and attracts many yachts. Although devastated by the 1953 earthquake, Vathi was reconstructed as it was and is considered a 'traditional settlement' of Greece. One building that survived the quake is the mansion of the Drakolis family, who brought the first steamship to Greece, which they named the *Ithaka*. The **Archaeology Museum** is behind the Mentor Hotel, housing a collection of vases, offerings and other objects, many dating from Homeric times. In the **church of the Taxiarchos** an icon of Christ is attributed to the young El Greco. An annual conference on Homer, the International Odessa Congress, has taken place in Vathi since 1981.

West of Vathi it's an hour's walk to the **Cave of the Nymphs** or Marmarospilia (signposted) where Odysseus hid the gifts of King Alcinoos. The cave is especially interesting for the hole in the roof—'the entrance of the gods'—which permitted the smoke of the sacrifices to rise to heaven. The cave has a few stalactites—bring a torch. Below is the **Bay of Dexia**, where the Phaeacians put the sleeping Odysseus on shore. South of Vathi above the little beach and islet of **Perapigadia**, flows the **Fountain of Arethusa**. According to the myth, Arethusa wept so much when her son Corax was killed that she turned into a spring and it was here that Odysseus, disguised as a beggar, first met the faithful Eumaeus. The water flows from the rock Corax—also mentioned by Homer—and is good to drink, although beware that it has a reputation for increasing the appetite.

The only other real village in the south of Ithaca is **Perachori**, also within walking distance of Vathi. Perachori lies in the island's most fertile region and dates from the Venetians, although the first houses were built in **Paleochora**, where you can see the ruins of the fortified houses and churches, one minus its roof but still adorned with fading Byzantine frescoes. In Perachori the villagers will show you which path to take. Another road from the village goes up to the 17th-century **Monastery of the Taxiarchos** near the top of Mt Stefano. Although not all that much remains, the views from the monastery and the road are good. In August Perachori hosts a wine festival.

North of Vathi

Ithaca has an hourglass figure, with a waist only 500m wide. This narrow mountain stretch is called **Aetos**. There is a beach in the bay below and at **Piso Aetos** in the west. Overlooking the bay is Schliemann's **Castle of Odysseus**, actually the citadel of the 8th-century BC town of Alalcomenes. Impressive Cyclopean walls and the foundations of a temple remain.

Just north of Aetos is the so-called **Field of Laertes** or Agros, from where a road ascends the slopes of Mt Neritos (formerly Mt Korifi—Ithaca is slowly reclaiming its Homeric names) to the **Monastery of Kathara**, founded in 1696. From the monastery you can see the Gulf of Patras, and even though the monastery is now abandoned, its church of the **Panayia** is kept open in the summer for visitors to see the frescoes and icon attributed to St Luke. From Kathara the road continues to **Anogi**, passing many large and unusually-shaped boulders. The village retains some Venetian ruins, including a campanile and another church dedicated to the **Panayia** with very old frescoes.

The second and better road from Agros follows the west coast. At Ag. Ioannis, just opposite Kefalonia, is a lovely, seldom-used beach, with many trees. **Levki**, the small village to the north, was an important base and port for the resistance movement during the war, and when it was destroyed by the 1953 earthquake, Britain officially adopted it and helped to rebuild it. Further north is **Stavros**, the most important village in the north, overlooking lovely **Polis Bay** ('city bay'), its name referring to the Byzantine city of Ierosalem, which sank into it during an earthquake in the 10th century. A bust of Odysseus in the centre of Stavros looks out over the bay, which has one of Ithaca's more popular beaches. The **Cave of Louizos** on the bay was an ancient cult sanctuary, where archaeologists found a number of items dating back to the Mycenaean age; one of the gods worshipped here was Odysseus (unfortunately the cave and path to it have collapsed). By common consent Odysseus' palace was located at **Pilikata**, just north of Stavros. Although the ruins you see on the site are of a Venetian fort, excavators have found evidence underneath of buildings and roads dating back to the Neolithic era. Some of the finds from Pilikata and the Cave of Louizos are in the small but interesting **Stavros Archaeological Museum** on the Platrithias road (*open 9–2*). The site also fits the Homeric description almost perfectly, in sight of 'three seas' (the bays of Frikes, Polis and Aphales) and 'three mountains' (Neritos, Marmacas and Exogi).

North of Stavros, **Frikes** is a tiny fishing village and port for Fiskardo in Kefalonia and Vassiliki in Lefkas, as well as for daily caiques to Vathi, and a popular stopping-off point for flotilla yachts. There's a new hotel here and rooms and tavernas, as there are in nearby **Kioni**, one of Ithaca's prettiest villages, which has the better beaches. Kioni means 'column', and an ancient one still stands on the altar in the village church. In **Platrithias**, the centre of a group of small settlements north of Stavros, there's a small **ethnographic museum**, at Kolieri. This fertile area is one of the most pleasant on the island; it was here that King Odysseus was ploughing his field when he was dragged off to Troy by the Achaeans, never suspecting he'd be gone for 20 years.

Festivals

15 August, Platrithias; 24 June, Ag. Ioannis, at Kioni; mid-August to mid-September, theatre and cultural festival at Vathi; 5–6 August, Sotiros at Stavros; 8 September, Kathara Monastery; 1 May, Taxiarchos and August wine festival, Perachori.

Ithaca as a whole has very little accommodation—four hotels, two of which are in Vathi. Most modern and most expensive is the **Hotel Mentor**, class B, in Vathi on Georgiou Drakouli Street, © 32 433, a bit out of the centre, on the far side of the bay. A bit less dear and more convenient is the **Odysseus**, also in the B category, © 32 381. Although C class, the **Nostos Hotel**, at Frikes, has high rates—7500 dr., which is on a par with the Mentor, © 31 644. Less expensive, but get there early in the summer to find a room, is the **Pension Enoikiazomena** behind the town hall, on a narrow alley off Odysseus Street. The rooms are old but charming; try to get one looking out over the bay. There are also a few rooms to rent, here and in Perachori, Kioni and around Stavros.

Eating Out

In the centre of Vathi, near the main square, is **Trexandiri**, a restaurant serving good local food and, 800m from town, **Palio Karavo** is a favourite, especially for fish (2000 dr.). Both the Mentor and Odysseus hotels have good restaurants.

Kalamos and Kastus

Kalamos and Kastus, two islands off Meganisi, near Mitikas on the mainland, are under the jurisdiction of Ithaca. Kalamos, the larger one, is connected once a week to Sami, Ithaca, the port Astakos and Meganisi, as well as Nidri and Vassiliki on Lefkas. There is also a more frequent service from Mitikas. There are three small fishing villages on its rocky coast: Kalamos, Episkopi, and Kefali. Only two or three families live on Kastus, now unable to care for all the vineyards which once produced a fine wine.

Kefalonia

Mountainous and lacking the voluptuous lushness of Zakynthos and Corfu, Kefalonia may be the largest of the Ionian islands but supports only 30,000 people, many of whom live in Athens in the winter. Kefaloniotes are among Greece's most famous emigrants (one, Constantine Yerakis, went on to make a fortune in the British East India Company and become Regent of Siam), and it's

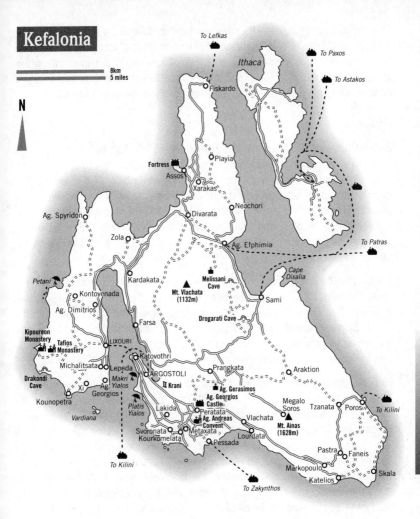

Kefalonia

8km
5 miles

N

To Lefkas
To Paxos
To Astakos

Ithaca

Fiskardo

Playia

Fortress
Assos

Xarakas

Neochori

Ag. Spyridon

Ag. Efphimia

To Patras

Divarata

Zola

Petani

Kardakata

Melissani Cave

Cape Dixalia

Kontoyenada

Mt. Vlachata (1132m)

Ag. Dimitrios

Sami

Farsa

Drogarati Cave

Kipoureon Monastery
Tafios Monastery
LIXOURI
Katovothri

Michalitsata
Lepeda

Prangkata

Araktion

Drakondi Cave
Xi
Makri Yialos
ARGOSTOLI
Il Krani

Ag. Gerasimos

Ag. Georgios Castle

Megalo Soros

Tzanata

Poros

To Kilini

Kounopetra
Georgios
Platis Yialos

Lakida
Peratata
Ag. Andreas Convent

Vlachata

Mt. Ainas (1628m)

Vardiana

Svoronata
Metaxata
Kourkomelata

Lourdata

Pastra

Faneis

Pessada

Markopoulo

Skala

To Kilini

Katelios

To Zakynthos

not uncommon to meet someone whose entire family lives in Canada, Australia or the United States: if the tourist boom has had a positive social benefit, it's that more people can make a living on their beautiful but untamed island. Kefaloniotes are friendly, easy-going people, and have the reputation of being Greece's worst blasphemers.

Although the earthquake in 1953 destroyed many of Kefalonia's grand old houses it has many charms to woo its visitors: fine beaches (one of which, Myrton, is perhaps the most dramatic in all of Greece), two of the country's loveliest caves, and great pine forests to picnic in and walk through, with many splendid views. Because Kefalonia is so large, it is easy to escape the summertime crowds.

History

Recent finds date the first Kefaloniotes to at least 50,000 BC and perhaps earlier; Fiskardo man, as the archaeologists have dubbed him, has proved to have many similarities with his peers in western Sicily and Epirus. The island is also exceptionally rich in its Mycenaean finds. Although the name Kefalonia does not occur in Homer, it is believed that the 'glittering Samos' of the *Odyssey* refers to Kefalonia's mountains, and that the island may well have been part of the kingdom of Odysseus, and certainly the home of many of Penelope's ill-mannered suitors.

Historically the first reference to Kefalonia describes its four city-states: Sami, the most powerful, Pali, Krani and Pronnoi. Hesiod refers to a renamed sanctuary of Zeus which stood on the top of Mt Ainos. Little else, however, is known of the 'Kefalonian Tetrapolis' until the Roman invasion, when the besieged Sami held out heroically for four months before the inevitable defeat, and the equally inevitable sale of its citizens into slavery.

In 1085, the Norman Duke Robert Guiscard of Sicily unsuccessfully besieged the Byzantine forts of the island and died of fever in the village that has taken his name—Fiskardo. If the Kefaloniotes breathed a sigh of relief then, it was too soon; for the next 800 years the island, like its sisters, was to become the plaything of the Normans, of Venice, the Vatican, and a motley assortment of dukes and counts in need of a tax income. Most famous of its occupiers was the pirate Count Matteo Orsini, who lived at the end of the 12th century. In 1483 the Turks captured the island, but lost it again in the early 1500s when Venice and Spain under the Gran Capitan, Gonzalo Fernández de Córdoba, besieged and captured the fort of Ag. Georgios and slaughtered the Turkish garrison.

After this the fortress was repaired and the town nearby became the Venetian capital. A huge earthquake caused heavy damage to Ag. Georgios, and by the 18th century it was abandoned, and Argostoli became the new capital. In 1823 Lord Byron showed up on Kefalonia (along with a retinue including his faithful Venetian gondolier Tita) as an agent of the Greek Committee in London before going to die a pathetic death from fever in Missolonghi. During the British occupation of the Ionian islands, the Kefaloniotes demanded Greek union more stridently than anyone else, and many nationalist leaders were imprisoned there. Ioannis Metaxas, prime minister-dictator of Greece from 1936 to 1941, came from Kefalonia, and for all his faults has gone down in history for saying 'No' to Mussolini's ultimatum at the beginning of the Second World War—celebrated nationally in November as *Oxi* ('No') day. In 1943, the Italian occupiers of the island joined forces with the EAM (Greek National Liberation Front) and for seven days fought the invading Germans. Three thousand of the Italians who were forced to surrender died in the subsequent mass executions ordered, it is said, by Hitler himself.

Connections

By air: daily flights from Athens, several a day in summer, and weekly summer flights to Zakynthos; frequent charters from British cities. The Olympic Airways office is in Argostoli, at Rokou Vergoti 1, © (0671) 28 808/881.

By sea: There are six ports, the main ones being Sami, and Argostoli. Ferries run daily from Sami to Ithaca, Lefkas, Patras and Brindisi, twice a week with Piraeus, Corfu and Ancona, once a week with Crete, Samos and Kuşadasi; every half hour from Argostoli to Kilini, on the Peloponnese, daily from Fiskardo to Ithaca and Lefkas, Ag. Efthimia to Ithaca and Astakos, on the mainland, Pessada to Skinari on Zakynthos, and two a day from Poros to Kilini.

By bus: From Athens, three times a day.

Around Kefalonia: Bus services to the rest of the island have been improved and next to the KTEL station on the waterfront there is a local tourist office to help you plan excursions. Many taxi drivers specialize in trips around the island, and caiques go to the more popular beaches. There is a car ferry across the Gulf of Argostoli six times a day from Argostoli to Lixouri.

Tourist Information

NTOG, Argostoli (0671) 22 248.
Tourist police, *see* regular police, Argostoli (0671) 22 200.

When Kefalonia was so badly damaged by the earthquake in 1953—only Fiskardo, in the extreme north, survived unscathed—the wealthy emigrants of the island donated large sums of money for the reconstruction of its villages. A fair portion of their money has gone to rebuilding the island's capital **Argostoli** (pop. 10,000), situated on a thumb of the great bay in the south. Part of this bay is so shallow that the British built the **Drapanos Bridge** over it, with its many low arches and commemorative obelisk that considerably shortens the journey to the other side of the bay. The port of Argostoli is especially safe and used for winter berthing of yachts and larger ships.

Argostoli has more public buildings than most island capitals, nearly all grouped around the large, central **Plateia Vallanou**. Pre-earthquake Argostoli was famous for its bell towers, some of which have been rebuilt—don't miss the German Expressionist tower of the Catholic church near the square. Two museums are nearby: the **Archaeology Museum** contains a room of Mycenaean finds—bronze swords and gold jewellery, coins from the four ancient cities of Kefalonia, and a bronze bust of a man from the early 3rd century BC that's startlingly modern. The **Koryalenios Historical and Folklore Museum** in the basement of the library on Ilia Zervou St contains the Venetian records of the island, icons, a traditional bedroom and other ethnographic items.

There are two sandy beaches south of Argostoli, the organized **Platis Yialos** and the free **Makri Yialos**. A pleasant walk along **Lassi**, the little peninsula north of Argostoli, leads to one of Kefalonia's more peculiar features—the **Katavothri** or swallow holes, where the sea is sucked into two large tunnels under the ground. No one knew where the water emerged until 1963, when Austrian geologists poured a vast quantity of dye into the water. Fifteen days later the dye appeared in the lake of the Melissani cave and at Karavomylos, near Sami, on the other side of the island. The sea mills that harnessed the rushing water, which were destroyed by the earthquake, have since been reconstructed.

On the other side of the peninsula is the lovely **lighthouse of Ag. Theodoros**, reconstructed in its rotunda of columns. On the other side of Argostoli, above the lagoon formed by the Drapanos Bridge and up off the road to Sami are the massive 7th-century BC walls of the acropolis of ancient **Krani**.

Lixouri and Western Kefalonia

Across the bay from Argostoli is the capital's longstanding rival, **Lixouri**, Kefalonia's second city, all new houses on wide streets and in itself not terribly interesting. In the central square near the waterfront stands a **statue of poet Andreas Laskaratos**, a local man of letters of the 19th century, remembered in particular for his dislike of the church. He was a poor man with a large family to support, and he kept heckling the priests so much that they finally excommunicated him—in Greek *aforismos*, meaning that the body will not decompose after death. When Laskaratos found out he hurried home, collected his children's decomposing shoes and returned to the priest, asking him to please excommunicate the footwear, too. You can get a sense of what pre-earthquake Lixouri was like on the west end of town at the **Iakovatos Mansion**, a rare survival and now a library and icon museum.

Lixouri is on the large westerly peninsula of Kefalonia that once formed part of the ancient city of Pali. There are beaches at **Michalitsata** and **Lepeda**, both sandy, and **Ag. Georgios** further south, a long stretch of golden sand most easily reached by caique. Just south of it the famous **Kounopetra** once created the optical illusion of opening and closing; the earthquake, however, fouled up the magic, and likewise destroyed the houses on the pretty, deserted **Vardiana islet** off the coast. The peninsula is shot full of caves: the most interesting, **Drakondi Spilio**, can be reached from the monastery of **Ag. Paraskevi Tafion**. Another monastery, **Kipoureon**, perched on the west cliffs, has spectacular views and overnight rooms. South of Manzavinata there's another fine beach, **Xi**, a long crescent of reddish sand. North of Lixouri there are more beaches: **Ag. Spyridon** near town and safe for children and **Petani**, pretty and quiet and rarely crowded. Even more remote—accessible by a minor road—is another beach called **Ag. Spyridon**, a stretch of sand tucked into the northernmost tip of Pali peninsula.

Southeast of Argostoli: the Livatho and Mt Ainos

Most of Kefalonia's rural population lives in the fertile region of valleys and rolling hills called the Livatho. At one village, **Metaxata**, Byron rented a house for four months in 1823 and finished his satirical rejection of romanticism, *Don Juan* while dithering over what to do as the representative of the London Committee, while each Greek faction fighting for independence jostled for the poet's attention—and especially his money. Nearby **Kourkomelata** was rebuilt by the wealthy Kefaloniote shipowner Vergotis; everything is as bright, new and pastel-coloured as a suburb of California.

On the road from Metaxata to Travliarata is the convent of **Ag. Andreas**, its bizarre prize possession the sole of St Andrew's foot. The quake of 1953 shook loose the whitewash in the interior of the church, revealing frescoes that date back to 1700 and have now been restored. Above the church looms the **Castle of Ag. Georgios**, and the town that until 1757 was the capital of Kefalonia. Most of the impressive ruins date from the early 16th century, when the citadel was rebuilt by Nikolaos Tsimaras. Held by the Byzantines, Franks, Turks and, after the fierce siege of 1500, the Venetians, it retains most of its walls, a ruined Catholic church, some forgotten coats-of-arms, and a bridge built by the French during their occupation. The castle commands a wonderful view of the surrounding plains and mountains; check opening hours at the tourist office.

To the east lies the green **plain of Omalos** and the **monastery of Ag. Gerasimos**, containing the body of the patron saint of the island. If 50 per cent of Corfiots are named Spiros after St Spyridon, then 50 per cent of the Kefaloniotes are named Gerasimos after their saint, whose speciality is intervening in mental disturbances, especially if the afflicted keeps an all-night vigil at his church on 20 October, his feast day. Architecturally, the monastery is most notable for its grotesque and ungainly bell tower. From the Argostoli–Sami road a branch leads off to Megalos Soros, the highest point of majestic **Mt Ainos**, at 1628m the loftiest in the Ionian islands. Before the arrival of Venetian shipbuilders the mountain was blanketed with the unique Kefalonian black pine—*Abies cefalonica*—so dense that the Venetians called Ainos the 'Black Mountain'. In 1962 what had survived of the forest was declared a national park, and it's still impressive to stroll among the tall, scented trees seemingly on top of the world; on a clear day the Peloponnese, Zakynthos, Ithaca, Lefkas, the Gulf of Patras and even Corfu are spread out below as if on a great blue platter.

The Southeast Coast: Beaches and the Virgin's Snakes

The south coast of Kefalonia, bursting with good sandy beaches, has become the island's tourism magnet. **Afrata, Trapezaki** and **Lourdata** (the longest and most crowded) have good beaches, while **Katelios** is a pretty place with springs, greenery and a beach, and becomes more popular every year, as does **Skala**, boasting another long beach. Near Skala a Roman villa was excavated, with 3rd-century mosaic floors, portraying Envy being devoured by wild beasts and two men making sacrifices to the gods. To the north of Skala a 7th-century BC temple of Apollo has also been discovered, though most of its stones were used to build the nearby chapel of Ag. Georgios.

Just inland, Kefalonia's most unusual religious event takes place in the village of **Markopoulo**. On 15 August, small harmless snakes 'inoffensive to the Virgin Mary' with little crosses on their heads, suddenly appear in the village streets. Formerly they slithered to the church, went inside and mysteriously disappeared near the Virgin's icon. Nowadays, to keep them from being run over, the villagers collect them in glass jars and bring them to the church, where they are released after the service and immediately disappear as they did in the past. Although sceptics believe that the church is simply along the route of the little snakes' natural migratory trail, the faithful point out that the snakes fail to appear when the island is in distress—as during the German occupation and in the year of the earthquake.

The road north, between Skala and **Poros** has been improved but is still narrow and difficult, although worth the trouble for the scenery and the pretty 'Poros Gap'. Because of its direct connection with Kilini, Poros is rapidly developing as the island's major resort area.

North Kefalonia: Caverns and Castles

Sami, the port for ships to Patras and Italy, is a growing resort in its own right, with beaches and a campsite, although the town itself is not very interesting. On the two hills behind the port are the **walls of ancient Sami**, where the citizens put up a heroic resistance to the Romans in 187 BC. Sami is also the best base for visiting Kefalonia's magnificent grottoes: **Drogarati cave**, near the hamlet of Haliotata, is a fairyland of orange and yellow stalactites and stalagmites; one of its great chambers has such fine acoustics that in the summer concerts are held there. The other, steep-sided **Melissani** ('purple cave') is a half-hour's walk from Sami; small boats wait to paddle you across its mysterious salt water lake (supplied by the swallow holes near Argostoli), immersing you in a vast shimmering play of blue and violet colours, caught by the sun filtering through a hole in the roof 30m overhead. *Both caves open 8–7 in summer, but close after October.* There are other, undeveloped caves in the vicinity of Sami, many with lakes and dangerous, precipitous drops, best of which is **Anglaki cave**, near Poulata.

Ag. Efphimia, the port for Ithaca and Astakos, also has a harbour for yachts and a hotel. Continuing up to the northernmost tip of Kefalonia, tiny **Fiskardo** derives its name from a mispronunciation of Robert Guiscard, who died there and was buried in a cairn (by the hotel). Some of Fiskardo's Venetian houses survived the 1953 earthquake, a poignant reminder of the handsome architecture Kefalonia once had; some have been fixed up for guests (*see* below).

South of Fiskardo, on the Argostoli road, is the magnificent castle of **Assos** set on a small peninsula, toy-sized from the lofty mountain road. It was built by the ancient Greeks and the Venetians restored it and sent a proveditor to govern it. On one of the harbours formed by the peninsula is the little fishing village of Assos, once full of sleepy charm, now unfortunately 'discovered' in a big way. Just to the south of it lies the superb beach of **Myrton**, embraced by sheer cliffs, spectacularly snow-white against a sea so blue it hurts.

Festivals

16 August and 20 October, Ag. Gerasimos; 15 August, Panayias at Markopoulo; 23 April, Ag. Georgios; 21 May, Ag. Konstantinos near Argostoli; carnival celebrations on the last Sunday and Monday before Lent; Easter festival in Lixouri; 21 May, Festival of the Radicals (celebrating union with Greece) in Argostoli; 23 June, Ag. Ioannis, at Argostoli; first Saturday after 15 August, Robola festival of wine in Fragata.

(0671–)

Where to Stay

expensive

On the beach at Lassi, there's the A class **Méditerranée**, the island's pride and joy, with all mod cons and air conditioned rooms, and offering a variety of land and sea sports, but its high summer rates will have you reaching for your fattest credit card, ℂ 28 761. On the beach Platis Yialos there's the **White Rocks**, another A class hotel-bungalow complex with air conditioning and other assorted comforts, ℂ 23 167.

moderate

Hotels in Argostoli can be surprisingly expensive; an example is the class C Cefalonia Star at 50 Metaxa St, ℂ 23 180, at 8000 dr. in season. Alternatively there's the Regina, two streets up from the waterfront at 24 Vergoti, for a little less, ℂ 23 557. In Sami there are more rooms to rent and two decent, clean hotels, the Ionion near the ferry, ℂ (0674) 22 035, and the Kyma, ℂ 22 064. On a more realistic level in Lassi is the C class Irilena, ℂ 23 172. In bijou Fiskardo, where everybody likes to stay, four typical houses have been renovated by the NTOG; for reservations, write to Paradosiakos Ikismos Fiskardou, Kefalonia, ℂ (0674) 51 398. There are two pensions, which are renovated and done out in traditional style, the Filoxenia, ℂ 51 487, and the Fiskardona, ℂ 51 484, and self-contained apartments for rent—Stella, ℂ 51348, and Kaminakia, ℂ 51 578. Although used by tour operators, the Summery in Lixouri, ℂ 91 771, is a pleasant place to stay.

cheap

In Argostoli you can get basic rooms at **Hara**, 87 Leof. Vergoti, ℂ 22 427, and **Parthenon**, 4 Zakynthou, ℂ 22 246. Simple accommodation may also be found in Lixouri, Poros, Lassi, Skala, Ag. Efthimia and Fiskardo. There's a **campsite** near Sami on Karavomilos beach, 1km from town and near Argostoli at Fanari, 2km from town.

Eating Out

In Sami there are two tavernas side by side on the waterfront, **Saoulis** and **Port Sami**, both serving fish, regular Greek dishes and some local specialities (meat pie and octopus pie); the latter has a delicious rosé retsina. Count on 1500–2000 dr. for a meal at either. In a back street in Argostoli is the **Captain's Table**, one of the finest vernacular restaurants in Kefalonia; it's virtually undiscovered by tourists, but a fashionable crowd of Greeks head there for the regional cooking. **Kaliva** has an attractive garden to match its pleasant prices, and is popular with tourists and locals alike. On the waterfront the **Kalafate** is also good and reasonable. In Lassi the most popular spot is the **Ambassador**, for its excellent Greek food, garden and prices. Fiskardo, which is used to loads of yachtsmen dropping in, boasts a fine fish restaurant in the harbour, **Dendrinos** (3000 dr.), and it's worth searching out **Nicolas' Garden** (if Nicolas doesn't find you first), hidden up a narrow alley in the middle of the village; excellent food in a relaxing setting (2500 dr.). In Assos there isn't much choice—most people go to **Kokolis**. In Lixouri **Akroyiali** has good fish in season, and it doesn't cost an arm and a leg. There is a selection of little tavernas in Poros and Skala. Kefalonia is an important island for quality Greek wines; the dry white, Robola of Kefalonia, is the best-known, but the tiny producer Gentilini is one of Greece's most

innovative wine-makers, and highly regarded internationally for dry whites. You can buy Gentilini bottles in good restaurants and in off-licences.

Kythera

The opening of the Corinth canal doomed any commercial importance Kythera once had by virtue of its position between the Ionian and Aegean seas. Today, unless you take the small plane from Athens, the island is rather difficult to reach. It has so lost its connections with its sister Ionian islands far to the northwest that politically it now belongs to Attica and is administered from Piraeus. In this century the population has decreased by more than half, most of them emigrating to the other side of the world; some 100,000 people of Kytheran origin now live in Australia ('Big Kythera' according to the locals, when other Greeks call their island the Kangaroo Colony). All the emigrants who can, come back to Kythera in the summer, constituting its main tourist rush. With only a few hotels and rooms to let, the island is one of the quietest in Greece, and the non-Aussies who do visit are usually of the hardy Hellenophile type anxious to escape their own countrymen, or the wealthy who have scattered their villas all over Kythera. The island is not without its charms, although it hardly matches the shimmering luxuriance of Watteau's *Pèlerinage à l'Ile de Cythère*.

History

When Zeus castrated his father, Cronus, then ruler of the world, he cast the bloody member into the sea. This gave birth to Aphrodite, the goddess of love, who rose out of the foam at Kythera, but finding it small she moved to Paphos, Cyprus, and was called either the Cypriot or the Kytherian. An ancient sanctuary dedicated to Aphrodite on Kythera was the most sacred of all such temples in Greece.

Aphrodite was known as Astarte by Kythera's first settlers, the Phoenicians, who came for the murex shells, from which they extracted a purple dye to colour royal garments, and from which the island derived its other early name, Porphyrousa. The Minoans, the first in Greece to worship Aphrodite, made Kythera a central trading station, for its location at the crossroads between Crete and the mainland, and the Aegean and Ionian Seas. The location was also convenient for aggressors: Kythera was invaded 80 times in recorded history. Particularly frightful were the visits of the Saracens from Crete, so ferocious in the 10th century that the island was abandoned altogether until Nikephoros Phokas won Crete back for Byzantium.

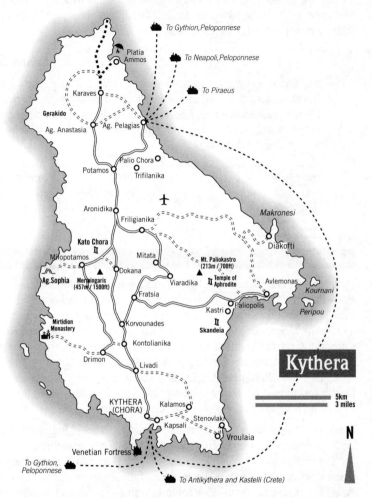

To Gythion, Peloponnese

To Neapoli, Peloponnese

To Piraeus

Platia Ammos

Karaves

Gerakido

Ag. Anastasia

Ag. Pelagias

Palio Chora

Potamos

Trifilanika

Aronidika

Friligianika

Makronesi

Kato Chora

Mitata

Mt. Paliokastro (213m / 700ft)

Diakofti

Milopotamos

Dokana

Mermingaris (457m / 1500ft)

Viaradika

Temple of Aphrodite

Avlemonas

Ag. Sophia

Fratsia

Kournani

Mirtidion Monastery

Korvounades

Kastri

Paliopolis

Peripou

Kontolianika

Skandeia

Drimon

Livadi

Kythera

KYTHERA (CHORA)

Kalamos

5km
3 miles

Stenovlak

Kapsali

Vroulaia

N

Venetian Fortress

To Gythion, Peloponnese

To Antikythera and Kastelli (Crete)

The rulers of Kythera in the Middle Ages were the Eudhaemonoyannis family from Monemvassia. The Venetians occupied the island in 1204, but with the help of Emperor Michael Palaeologos, Kythera was regained for the Eudhaemonoyannis, and for long years it served as a refuge for Byzantine nobles, especially after the Turks grabbed the Peloponnese. However, in 1537, Barbarossa stopped at Kythera on his way home from the unsuccessful siege of Corfu and destroyed the island. The Venetians occupied the island again in the 15th century and called it

'Cerigo', the name by which it is known in the old history books. The Turks took over again in the early 18th century; in 1864 it was ceded to Greece by the British with the rest of the Ionian islands.

Connections

At least one flight a day from Athens; hydrofoil five times a week from Gythion, three times a week from Piraeus, Hydra, Spetses and Monemvassia; regular ferry boat from Neapolis daily, five times a week with Gythion, twice a week with Monemvassia, Crete and Piraeus, once a week with Antikythera.

Tourist Police

See regular police, © (0733) 31 206.

Chora

Kythera, or **Chora**, the capital of Kythera, is a pretty blue and white village, 275m above the port of Kapsali, impressively guarded by a fortress finished by the Venetians in 1503. Chora's location was supposedly selected by pigeons, who took the tools of the builders from a less protected site. Ten old **Venetian mansions** in Chora still retain their coats-of-arms, and a small **museum**, generally open in the mornings, contains artefacts dating back to Minoan times. Below, a 20-minute walk down the hill, **Kapsali** has a large house with rooms to let owned by one Emmanuel Comnenus (probably a descendant of the Byzantine nobles who fled to Kythera from Mystra), a few restaurants and two beaches.

Buses leave Chora about once a day for the major villages of the island. Alternatively there are taxis which charge a set fee for different excursions. **Kalamos**, just east of Chora, is within walking distance. One of its churches, Ag. Nikitis, has a pretty bell tower, and there is a taverna by the square. A dirt road continues across the rugged landscape to **Vroulaia**, a pebble beach and taverna, where many people pitch their tents.

Northwest of Chora

From Chora the paved road heads north to **Livadi**, where once-golden wheat-fields have run wild from a lack of labour and there's a pretty bridge of 13 arches. Heading west from Livadi via Drimon is the important **Monastery of the**

Panayia Mirtidion with a tall carved bell tower, set on the wild west coast among cypresses, flowers and peacocks. The monastery is named for a golden icon of the Virgin and Child, whose faces are blackened with age—a sign of special holiness that attracts a huge number of pilgrims to the monastery on 15 August. Two small islets just offshore are said to be pirate ships that the Virgin turned to stone for daring to attack the monastery.

North of Drimon, **Milopotamos** is the closest thing to Watteau's vision of Kythera. It is the island's loveliest village, criss-crossed by tiny canals of clear water—so much water, in fact, that the toilet in the valley is in a constant state of flush. The stream valley through the middle of town is called the Neraida, or Nymph, and a good restaurant there has music and dancing at night. An old watermill lies along the path to the waterfall, surrounded by the ancient plane trees, flowers and banana plants; on quiet evenings you can hear the nightingales sing.

The ghost town **Kato Chora** lies just below Milopotamos within the walls of a Venetian fortress built in 1560. Above the gate there's a bas-relief of the lion of St Mark and a Latin inscription, welcoming you to a desolation of empty stone houses. By the sea below is the cave **Ag. Sophia**, at the end of a rugged, descending road. In the past the cave was used as a church, and inside there are frescoes and mosaics, as well as stalactites and stalagmites and small lakes that go on and on...; some say it tunnels all the way under Kythera to Ag. Pelagias. And at Ag. Pelagias a sign does indeed point down a rocky hill to a mysterious Ag. Sophia.

The East Coast

Skandeia was the port of the ancient town of Kythera, mentioned by Thucydides, and ruins of the settlement may be seen at the site now known as **Kastri**. The ancient town itself was above Paliopolis up at **Paliokastro**; here worshippers came to the ancient temple of Urania Aphrodite 'Queen of the Mountains' to pay their respects to the goddess. The Christians, however, destroyed the sanctuary to build the church of Ag. Kosmas (with the temple's Doric columns). All that remains at Paliokastro are the acropolis walls.

From Paliopolis the coastal road leads to **Avlemonas**, where the Minoans had a trading settlement dating from 2000 BC until the rise of the Mycenaeans. By the sea is a small octagonal fortress built by the Venetians, who left a coat-of-arms and a few rusting cannon inside. There is also a small beach.

Much further north is **Palio Chora** (or Ag. Dimitriou), the town built by the Eudhaemonoyannis clan in the Monemvassian style. High on the rocks, it was hidden from the sea—Barbarossa found it only by capturing the inhabitants and forcing them to tell him where it was. Beside the ruins of the fort is a terrible abyss down which mothers threw their children before leaping themselves, to avoid the Turks. Most of the island's ghost stories and legends are centred on this tragic place.

Palio Chora is near **Potamos**, which despite its name, has no river. It is the largest village in the north, all blue and white like Chora. It has a bank and an Olympic Airways office, and the largest building at the edge of town is the island's retirement home. At **Gerakido** to the northwest you can see yet another tower, this time built by the Turks in the early 18th century. From Karaves a by-road continues to the fine beach at **Platia Ammos**. **Ag. Pelagias**, Kythera's northern port and most pleasant resort, also has a long beach.

Elafonissos and Antikythera

From Ag. Pelagias you can see the islet **Elafonissos**, connected by ship once a week (or daily in the summer by caique from Neapolis). Its village is mostly inhabited by fishermen and sailors, although a new village, **Kata Nisso**, is under construction with a hotel, for little Elafonissos is endowed with two gorgeous sandy beaches a kilometre long, as yet hardly discovered by tourists.

Another islet, **Antikythera** (or Lious) lies to the south of Kapsali, nearly midway to Crete. Ships call once a week en route between Kythera and Crete. Fewer than 150 people live in Antikythera's two villages, Potamos and Sochoria, and the rest is very rocky with few trees; curiously, like west Crete, the island is slowly rising. By Potamos, ancient **Aigilia** has walls dating back to the 5th century BC.

Festivals

15 August, Panayias Mirtidion; 29–30 May, Ag. Trias at Mitata.

(*0735–*)

Where to Stay

expensive

When it comes to finding a place to stay on Kythera you may be hard-pressed. For families and longer stays there are furnished apartments in Kapsali, © 31 265, Ag. Pelagias, © 33 466, and at Pitsinades, © 33 570, with daily rates ranging from 8000 dr. to 18,000 dr., depending on the number of people. The **Raikos** pension in Kapsali is the island's biggest (24 rooms) and most expensive hotel accommodation, © 31 629, followed by the **Aphrodite** in Kapsali, © 31 328. There's one B class pension in Livadi, the **Aposperides**, © 31 790.

moderate–cheap

In Kythera town (Chora) there are small B class pensions **Keti**, © 31 318, and **Margarita** (no phone). Up in Ag. Pelagias the 10-roomed **Kytheria** pension, © 33 321, serves breakfast, and in Manitochori, **Ta Kythera** (again, another small pension) has clean, pleasant double rooms, © 31 563. Potamos has the pretty **Porfyra**, © 33 329, with eight rooms. Other than that there are a few rooms to be had at Ag. Pelagias, Potamos, Kythera town and Milopotamos.

Eating Out

Kapsali has the most in the way of restaurants, including the American-style **Kapsi Kamales**, where you can dine for around 2500 dr. For about the same price, well-prepared Greek dishes can be had at **Kamares tou Mayeira**, also in Kapsali. There are a number of typical, simple tavernas offering straightforward Greek food up in Chora, notably **Zorba's**, in the main street; there's also the restaurant in Milopotamos and in Ag. Pelagias a limited selection of tavernas.

Lefkas (Lefkada)

Lefkas (more popularly known in Greece by its genitive form Lefkada) was named for its white cliffs. It barely qualifies as an island; in ancient times Corinthian colonists dug what is now the 20m (66ft) wide Lefkas ship canal, separating the peninsula from the mainland. This is kept dredged by the Greek government and is easily crossed by a pontoon bridge; beyond the canal a series of causeways surrounds a large, shallow lagoon (salt is one of Lefkada's industries). A series of earthquakes—most recently in 1953—destroyed nearly all of the island's architectural interest. Lefkada is especially well known for the laces and embroideries produced by its women, many of whom keep a loom in the back room of their houses. Lefkada is gradually developing its tourist potential, in part based on the perfect conditions for windsurfing at Vassiliki. There's a fair amount of hotel and villa construction underway, but most of the holidaymakers are Greek.

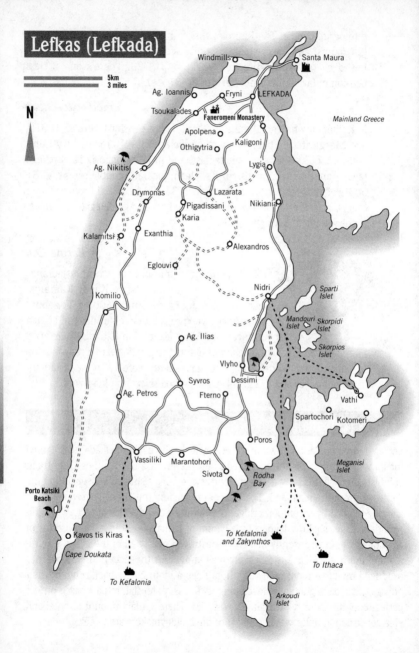

Lefkas (Lefkada)

5km
3 miles

N

Windmills
Santa Maura
Ag. Ioannis
Fryni
LEFKADA
Tsoukalades
Faneromeni Monastery
Mainland Greece
Apolpena
Kaligoni
Othigytria
Lygia
Ag. Nikitis
Drymonas
Lazarata
Nikiana
Pigadissani
Karia
Kalamitsi
Exanthia
Alexandros
Eglouvi
Nidri
Komilio
Sparti Islet
Mandouri Islet
Skorpidi Islet
Skorpios Islet
Ag. Ilias
Vlyho
Syvros
Dessimi
Vathi
Fterno
Spartochori
Kotomeri
Ag. Petros
Poros
Vassiliki
Marantohori
Meganisi Islet
Sivota
Rodha Bay
Porto Katsiki Beach
Kavos tis Kiras
Cape Doukata
To Kefalonia and Zakynthos
To Ithaca
To Kefalonia
Arkoudi Islet

History

Although inhabited at least as far back as the Early Bronze Age, Lefkada first enters the scene of recorded history in 640 BC, when it was colonized by the Corinthians. After digging the channel that gave Lefkada its island status, the Corinthians built a fort at the northern tip, near the mainland, throughout history the key to Lefkada. During the Peloponnesian War Lefkada sided with Sparta and was devastated twice, by the Corcyraeans and the Athenians. The ancient capital was near Themodern, and at the white cliffs of Cape Doukata stood a temple of Apollo, where the poet Sappho leapt to her death, in despair over an unrequited love. Another great moment in the island's history was the Battle of Aktium, which once and for all settled the claims of Augustus on the Roman Empire over those of Mark Anthony and Cleopatra. The Venetians built the original fortress of Santa Maura, a name they adopted for the whole of the island. When Constantinople fell in 1453, the mother of the last Emperor Constantinos XI, Helene Palaeologos, founded a monastery within the walls of Santa Maura. When the Turks took Lefkas in 1479, they turned the monastery into a mosque.

In 1500 the combined forces of Spain and Venice under the Gran Capitan Gonzales de Cordova captured Lefkas and Santa Maura in the name of Christianity, but the very next year Venice made a treaty with Turkey and returned the island. In 1684, Venetian nobleman Francesco Morosini, angry at losing his own fortress at Herakleon, Crete, was determined to win Lefkas back for Venice, and he did with the help of a great number of Ionian islanders. With the fall of Venice, the French and then the Russians took Lefkas, the latter establishing it as part of the Septinsular Republic. In 1807 the tyrant Ali Pasha of Epirus moved to take Lefkas, but was held back by forces under the Russian-appointed Secretary of State, Count John Capodistria, who is said to have sworn to the cause of an independent Greece with rebellious refugees on the island, among them Kolokotronis.

Connections

By road: bus connections with Athens (five times a day), Arta and Preveza; by car from Athens about six hours' drive, from Preveza about one hour's drive.

By air: flights twice a day from Athens and occasional charters from England to Aktion, 26km away on the mainland, and bus connection from the airport.

By sea: in summer, boats from Nidri and Vassiliki to Sami, Fiskardo and Poros (Kefalonia) and Kioni (Ithaca). Daily boat to Meganisi. The island's bus service from Lefkas town to the other villages is irregular and generally stops running mid-afternoon.

Tourist Police

See regular police, Lefkas town, © (0645) 22 346, Vassiliki, © 31 218 and Vlichos, © 95 207.

Lefkas Town

If you approach Lefkada from land, the thing you'll see is the massive **Fortress of Santa Maura**, dipping its feet in the sea near Arkanania on the mainland. Most of what stands dates from the Venetian and Turkish reconstructions. It survived the periodic earthquakes better than the capital **Lefkas** which collapsed in the last earthquake in 1948; the fragile upper storeys of its buildings are an antiseismic measure. Another unusual feature of the town are its iron bell towers, rearing up like oil derricks near the 18th-century Venetian churches. Solidly built of stone, the churches have survived the tremors; examples of the Ionian school of painting are in **Ag. Minas** and **Ag. Dimitrios**.

There are three small museums (*open daily*) in Lefkas town: the **Archaeology Museum**, housing mostly the finds made by Dörpfeld in Nidri; the **Icon Museum**, with works of the Ionian school, housed in the municipal library; and the **Lefkada Sound Museum**, at 29 Kalkani St, founded by a local collector and the only museum of its kind in Greece, with old gramophones sent over by relatives from the United States, records of Cantades and popular Greek songs of the 1920s, and one of the first discs recorded by a Greek company, 'Orpheon' of Constantinople, founded in 1914. There are also a number of antiques from Lefkada . A cemetery dating from 600 BC has recently been discovered on the outskirts of town, and archaeologists from all over Greece are swooping on the site.

Just above Lefkas is the 17th-century **Faneromeni Monastery**, rebuilt in the 19th century after a fire. It is a charming and serene place, with bird's-eye views over the town, lagoon and the walls of Santa Maura. There are pebbly beaches along the causeway, near the derelict windmills. The central bus station is on the waterfront, near the bridge, and buses to the coastal villages are frequent.

The East Coast

The rest of Lefkada still retains much of its rural charm, and it's not unusual to encounter an older woman still dressed in her traditional costume. A short distance from Lefkas town on a hill near the east shore are the ruins of ancient **Leukas**, the Corinthian city, although there's little to see except the walls and traces of a theatre. Further south is **Nidri**, one of Lefkada's small resort towns, looking out over the lovely wooded islets of **Mandouri, Sparti, Skorpidi** and **Skorpios**, the last belonging to the Onassis family. From the sea you can spy Aristotle's tomb and excursion boats now have permission to land on the beaches if no one is in residence. You may notice a little red caique taking over a small army of workers who maintain the island; Onassis stipulated in his will that they must be from Nidri. On the plain behind Nidri, Wilhelm Dörpfeld, who assisted Schliemann in the excavation of Troy, found a number of Bronze Age tombs that he believed proved his theory that Lefkas was the Ithaca of Homer. He died in 1940 and is buried near the house in which he lived, on the peninsula facing the town.

Sit at a café in Nidri at twilight—there's one so near the shore you may sit with your feet in the sea—and, to the sound of croaking frogs, watch Mandouri float above the horizon on a magic carpet of mist. The mansion on Mandouri belongs to the family of the poet Aristelis Valaoritis who, like Angellos Sikelianos, came from Lefkas and was inspired by Lefkada's mix of mainland and island cultures.

Vlyho, the next village south, is a quiet charmer and in walking distance of sandy Dessimi beach. From **Syvros**, one of the larger villages in the interior, you can climb to the cave **Karouha**, the largest on the island. **Poros** and **Sivota** (with several tavernas, rooms and pensions) are popular swimming places with the local people.

Vassiliki, Windsurfing and the Original Lover's Leap

Vassiliki is both a shady, charming village with beaches and one of the best places in Europe to windsurf. Shops there specialize in all types of boards. A gentle breeze blows up by mid-morning, perfect to teach beginners the fundamentals, and by mid-afternoon it's blowing strong for the experts; by evening, the wind, like a real gent, takes a bow and exits, allowing a pleasant dinner by the water's edge. From Vassiliki you can take a caique (or road from Komilio) to see the 60m white cliffs of **Cape Doukata**, the original Lover's Leap, where Sappho, rejected by Phaon, hurled herself into the sea below. Evidence suggests, however, that the leap was not always a fatal cure for unrequited love; like the divers of Alcapulco, priests serving at the temple of Apollo Lefkada (of which only the scantiest ruins remain) would make the jump safely as part of their cult, called *katapontismos*. Later, Romans rejected by their sweethearts would make the leap—with the precaution of strapping on feathers or even live birds and employing rescue parties to pull them out of the sea below. The white cliffs are a famous landmark for sailors; Byron's Childe Harold 'saw the evening star above Leucadia's far-projecting rock of woe' as he sailed past. Today, a lighthouse marks the historic spot. Also reachable by caique from Vassiliki is the beautiful and remote beach of **Porto Katsiki**, covered with brilliantly white pebbles.

Up the West Coast

The west coast of Lefkada is rocky and rugged as far as **Ag. Nikitis**, which has blossomed into a sizeable resort with a long beach and clean, if cold, water. Don't let your windsurfer run away with you, though—the odd shark fin has been spotted off the coast. Just south of here a new road allows access to **Kathisma**, a good place to swim with a snack bar on the beach. **Ag. Petros** is the prettiest village on this side of the island. In the interior there are several notable churches with frescoes, among them the Red Church (Kokkino Eklisia) in **Alexandros**, and the 15th-century church at **Othigytria**, its design incorporating Byzantine and Western influences.

Festivals

Carnival festivities, with a parade; in August, the Arts and Letters Festival and large International Folklore Festival, in Lefkas town; two weeks in mid-August, Ag. Spyridon, at Karia, when the people bring out their old costumes (Karia is well known for its hand-made lace and woven carpets); 30 May, Faneromeni Monastery; 11 November, Ag. Minas in Lefkas; 26 July, Ag. Paraskevi near Ag. Petros.

(*0645–*)

Where to Stay

expensive

In Lefkas town, on the waterfront overlooking the canal, is the **Xenia**, © (0645) 24 762, with compulsory half board in high season. More comfortable in the same price range is the **Hotel Lefkas**, © 23 916. In Ag. Nikitis the **Odyssia** is one of the island's nicest hotels, © 99 366. At Nikiana, between Lefkas town and Nidri, the **Porto Galini** provides luxurious furnished apartments, and watersports down on the beach, © 92 431.

Two km north of Nidri in Perigiali, **Scorpios** has studios and apartments for rent, and there's a pool, ✆ 92 452. Just outside Nidri, the **Athos** is a popular place, with pool, pleasant bar and Chinese food, ✆ 92 384.

moderate

Next door to the Hotel Lefkas is the **Niricos Hotel**, ✆ 24 132, also a class B. Less expensive and on the main drag is the small and ordinary **Byzantium Hotel**, ✆ 22 629. Down in Nidri the **Nidri Beach Hotel I and II** are run by the same family and have good views, ✆ 92 400. Good value in Vassiliki is the **Paradissos**, an E class, but some rooms come with private bath, ✆ 31 256. In Ag. Nikitis smart rooms with private bath and overlooking the sea are around 6000 dr.

cheap

Rooms in private homes on the island start at 2500 dr. In Nidri, Vlyho and especially in Vassiliki you can usually find a room without too much difficulty from 3000 dr. upwards. There are **campsites** at Dessimi Beach near Vlyho, at Poros Beach further south, and at Vassiliki.

Eating Out

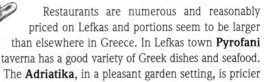

Restaurants are numerous and reasonably priced on Lefkas and portions seem to be larger than elsewhere in Greece. In Lefkas town **Pyrofani** taverna has a good variety of Greek dishes and seafood. The **Adriatika**, in a pleasant garden setting, is pricier but has some good Greek specialities and excellent service (2500 dr.). Eat at least once at **Kavos** on the beach at Nidri for the view and consistently good food for 1500–2000 dr. Just outside Nidri, **Haradiatika** is popular with locals for its good quality meat and *meze*. Vassiliki has a fine taverna on the beach, **Alex's**, serving some good English dishes and curries. Sivota has several tavernas on the beach, and you can pick your lobster from the sea cages; try the fish soup here.

Meganisi lies off the southeast coast of Lefkada. Ferries go there daily from Nidri, calling at **Vathi**, its port and largest settlement. It is a rocky islet but not without beauty. The only time when many people go there is for the *paniyiri* of Ag. Konstantinos on 21 May at the hamlet of Kotomeri. **Arkoudi**, another islet south of Lefkas, is uninhabited.

Paxos

Tiniest and yet one of the most charming islands in the Ionian Sea, Paxos and its little sister Antipaxos have long served as a kind of outlet from the mass package tourism and over-development of Corfu. Paxos (or Paxoi) is so small and so flat you can easily walk its 8km length in a day; its one road twists and turns through the immaculate groves of olives that brought the islanders most of their income before tourism. Paxos' olive oil is still considered among the best produced in Greece and has won many international medals. Besides the beauty of the silvery trees (there are some 300,000—each family owns at least 500) and the tidy stone walls, the little island has some of the friendliest people you'll find anywhere in Greece.

History

Paxos was happily shunned by history. What mention it received in antiquity referred to its seven sea caves—Homer mentions one, Ipparandi, describing it as having rooms of gold. In another cave the Greek resistance hero Papanikolaos hid and waylaid passing Italian ships in the Second World War, a trick unfortunately copied by German U-boats the following year.

Plutarch recounts an incident of great moment that took place off the shore of Paxos, at the beginning of the 1st century AD. Thamus, the Egyptian pilot of a ship sailing near the island, heard a voice call his name and say: 'When the ship comes opposite Palodes, you must announce the death of the Great God Pan.' When Thamus did so at the designated spot, great cries of lamentation arose. So the old gods were replaced with a new, marking the end—and the beginning—of a Great World Age.

Connections

Daily with Corfu, Brindisi (Italy), Igoumenitsa and Parga (on the mainland), also infrequent connections with Patras, Kefalonia and Ithaca. Connections are far less frequent in the off season. In the summer you may well be asked to have a room reservation before boarding a ferry to the island which is small, wooded, and fearful of campers and their fires.

Tourist Police

See regular police in Gaios, © (0662) 31 222.

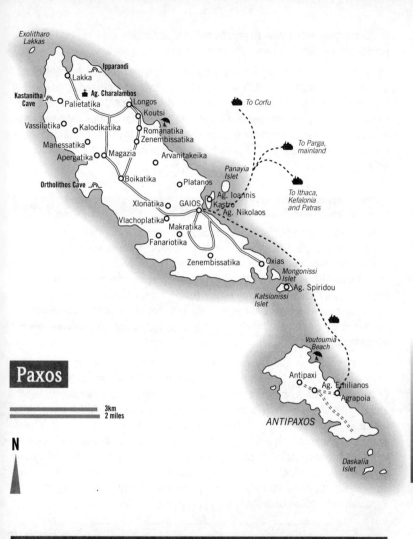

Paxos

3km
2 miles

N

Gaios

Gaios, the pretty little capital of the island, is named after a disciple of St Paul who brought Christianity to Paxos and is buried there. Most of the islanders live here, and it's where you'll find a small sandy beach and all of Paxos' facilities, including a tiny **aquarium** on the harbour-front. The streets of Gaios are fortunately too narrow for cars, although human traffic jams occur during the day in the summer, when day-trippers from Corfu and cruise ships sail into the little port; in the evening, however, the island regains its composure.

On a rocky islet facing the harbour is the well-preserved **Kastro Ag. Nikolaos**, built by the Venetians in 1423, and an old windmill, and beyond it, the islet of **Panayia**, which on 15 August is crowded with pilgrims. In the evening they come back to Gaios and dance all night in the village square. **Mongonissi**, another islet, is connected by caique—belonging to the family which owns a pretty little restaurant there—which brings customers over for dinner in the evening.

Sea Caves and Forests of Olives

Caiques may also be rented for a tour of Paxos' seven sea caves of brilliant blue. Most of these grottoes are located among the sheer cliffs on the western side of Paxos, including the impressive **Kastanitha**, 185m high. Another distinctive cave, **Ortholithos**, has a sentinel-like monolith at its entrance. It is possible to penetrate about 5m inside by caique. Homer's **Ipparandi** does not have the golden rooms he mentions, although it often shelters monk seals. **Grammatiko** is the largest cave of them all. When sailing around the island, you can also see the **Mousmouli Cliffs** and their natural bridge **Tripitos**.

The main road from Gaios across the island was donated by Aristotle Onassis, a great fan of Paxos. At its northern end is **Lakka**, a tiny port where the boats from Corfu usually call (connected by minibus with Gaios). Lakka has a small beach, and the Byzantine church in the village has particularly musical Russian bells, which you can ring if you find the villager with the key. The 19th-century **Grammatikou mansion** near Lakka is fortified with a tower. In **Boikatika** village the church Ag. Charalambos contains an old icon of the Virgin and in nearby **Magazia** are two churches of interest, Ag. Spyridon and Ag. Apostoli; the latter's churchyard affords an impressive view of the Eremitis cliffs. At **Apergatika** the Papamarkou mansion dates from the 17th century.

Festivals

Easter Monday procession from Gaios to Velliantitika; 15 August, Panayias; 11 August, Ag. Spyridon; 10 February, Ag. Charalambos.

expensive

Official accommodation is extremely limited, rather expensive, and block-booked by tour operators in the summer: a case in points the class B **Paxos Beach Bungalows**, ✆ 31 211, in Gaios, with pleasant, comfortable chalet bungalows near the beach, but these are only available in the off season.

moderate

Paxos has two E class hotels, the **Ilios**, ✆ 31 808, and **Lefkothea**, in Lakka, ✆ 31 807; again, they are both small, and fill up in season. Everyone else stays in private rooms, which are invariably pleasant, tidy and double, and average 4000–5000 dr.

Eating Out

Again, be prepared for prices a little above the norm. Restaurants and cafés take full advantage of the day-trippers who come from Corfu, and the yachting set berthed in Gaios. Take the caique to Mongonissi for the excellent restaurant there (2500–3000 dr.) and to while the day away on the beach. There are a handful of tavernas in Gaios such as the **Taka Taka** serving solid Greek fare and fish, the former reasonably priced, the latter about 3500 dr. for a meal. There is not much to choose between the tavernas in Longos, and in Lakka you can eat well and reasonably at **Sgarelios** and **Klinis**.

Antipaxos

South of Paxos lies tiny Antipaxos, with only a few permanent residents. From June until September four or five caiques leave Gaios daily for the 40-minute trip to its port **Agrapoia**. Although both Paxos and Antipaxos were created with a resounding blow of Poseidon's trident (the sea god thought that the gap between Corfu and Lefkas was a bit too large), the two islands are very different in nature. Rather than olive oil, Antipaxos produces good white and red wines, and instead of rocky sea caves, its coasts are graced with fine sandy beaches: **Voutoumia** and **Vrika** are 'softer than silk'. There is no accommodation on the islet, but those planning to stay should bring a sleeping bag, and be discreet. This could well be the uncontaminated paradise you've been seeking.

Zakynthos (Zante)

Of all their Ionian possessions the Venetians loved Zakynthos the most for its charm and natural beauty. *Zante, fiore di Levante*—'the flower of the East'—they called it, and built a city even more splendid than Corfu on its great semi-circular bay, all turned to dust and rubble by the earthquake of 1953. Nevertheless, the disaster did nothing to diminish the soft, luxuriant charm of the landscape and its fertile green hills and mountainsides, the valleys with their vineyards and currant vines, olive and almond groves and orchards, or the brilliant garland of flowers and beautiful beaches (the flowers are best in spring and autumn, a time when few foreigners visit the island). And if the buildings are gone, the Venetians left a lasting impression—many islanders have Venetian blood. On the other side of the coin, the once politically-progressive Zakynthos has bellied up to the trough of grab-the-money-fast tourism that doesn't do the island justice, to the extent of sabotaging efforts to preserve the beaches where the loggerhead turtles breed.

History

According to tradition, Zakynthos was named for its first settler, a son of Dardanus from Arcadia. Pliny refers to a cavern on its Mons Nobilis (now Mt Skopos), as the entrance to the underworld. According to Homer, the Zantiots fought under the command of Odysseus at the Trojan War, although their island later became an independent, coin-minting state which set up colonies throughout the Mediterranean, especially Saguntum in Spain, which was besieged and demolished by Hannibal. Levinus took the island for Rome in 214 BC, and when the inhabitants rebelled, he burnt all the buildings on Zakynthos. Uniting with the Aeolians, the Zantiots forced the Romans to leave, although in 150 BC Flavius finally brought the troublesome island under control.

In 844 the Saracens captured the island from their base in Crete, but the Byzantines were strong enough to expel them. The Norman–Sicilian pirate Margaritone took Zakynthos in 1182, and three years later made it part of the County Palatine of Kefalonia, first governed by Margaritone. One of his successors ceded the island to the Venetians in 1209, who kept the island for almost 350 years, although the Turks captured and pillaged it between 1479 and 1484. The aristocratic privileges of the Venetians and wealthy Zantiots caused so much resentment among the commoners that they rose up in 'the Rebellion of the Popolari' and took control of the island for four years. In the 17th century, many Cretan artists took refuge on the Venetian Zakynthos, and the island became the centre of the Ionian school of painting, producing artists like Doxaras, Koutouzis and Kantorinis. The song cult of the Cantades flourished as well and the island

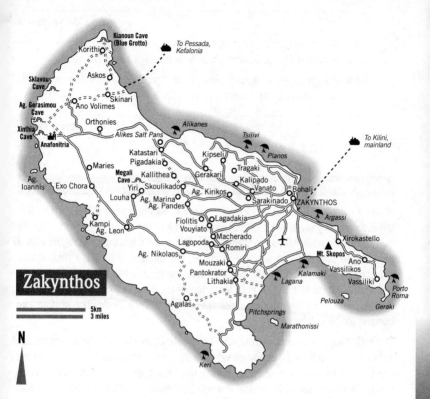

saw the birth of several poets: Ugo Foscolo (d. 1827), who wrote in Italian, and the nationalist poets Andreas Kalvos (d. 1867) and Dionysos Solomos (d. 1857); Solomos, 'the poet of the Greek War of Independence', was one of the first to write in Demotic Greek and composed the lyrics to the Greek National Anthem.

The Zantiots responded actively to the ideas of the French Revolution, forming their own Jacobin Club and destroying the hated rank of nobility. The Russians in 1798 forced the French garrison and the inhabitants to surrender, after a siege of months, and when the Septinsular Republic established aristocrats of its own, Zakynthos rebelled again in 1801. During the War of Independence many rebels on the mainland found asylum on the island before it joined Greece with its Ionian sisters in 1864.

By air: daily flights from Athens, two or three times a week with Kefalonia and Corfu. Several charters from major European cities.

By sea: ferry six or seven times a day from Kilini, twice a day from Kefalonia. Bus two or three times a day from Athens.

Tourist Police

1 Tzoulati, ℂ (0695) 22 200.

Zakynthos Town and the Eastern Peninsula

When the capital of the island, Zakynthos town, was rebuilt after the earthquake, the inhabitants gamely tried to incorporate some of the lost city's charm into the dull lines of modern Greek architecture. The town's setting gives it an added lustre—the graceful curve of the harbour, the ancient acropolis rising above, crowned by a castle, and to the right the unusual form of **Mt Skopos** ('look-out'), the Mons Nobilis of Pliny. A path leads to the top from the edge of the town; in the old days someone would make the 2-hour ascent every day to scan the horizon for pirate ships.

The city itself is long and narrow, and can easily be explored by horse-drawn cab or the cute double-pedal canopied vehicles for hire in the square. The streets are lined by arcades, all full of shops selling the local speciality, *mandolato* (white nougat with almonds). In central **Plateia Solomou** the 15th-century church of **Ag. Nikolaos** was pieced back together after the quake; here, too, is the **Neo-Byzantine Museum** (*8.30–3, closed Tues*) with paintings by the Ionian school, icons and other works of art salvaged from shattered churches across the island and a relief by neo-Classical sculptor Thorvaldsen dedicated to High Commissioner Maitland. Another museum, two streets up at Ag. Markou Square, is the **Solomos Museum**, near the mausoleums of Dionysos Solomos and Andreas Kalvos, with mementoes of the poets and other famous Zantiots, as well as photographs of the island before 1953. Little 17th-century **Kyra ton Angelous**, another reconstructed chapel, is near the Xenia Hotel. At the south end of town a huge new basilica houses the relics of the island's patron saint, **Ag. Dionysos**, and is filled with gold and silver ex-votos, and frescoes by Cozzara, a student of Tiepolo.

Looming over the town is the well-preserved **Venetian Kastro**, an hour's walk from Plateia Solomou. It's an easier haul than tramping up Mt Skopos, and rewards with views not only of Zakynthos, but of the Peloponnese and the Bay of Navarino, where on 20 October 1827 the most famous battle of modern Greece was fought between the Turco-Egyptian navy and the Anglo-Franco-Russian fleet, leading directly to Greek independence. On the north edge of town is the old **British cemetery**.

The town beach isn't all that good—better to take a bus to the beaches on the eastern peninsula: **Argassi** under Mt Skopos, with a long line of hotels and tavernas along its waterfront; **Porto Zorro** (pension and taverna); **Vassiliki** (rooms and camping available) and the charming, pine-shaded sandy strand at **Porto Roma**, but bear in mind that because of the infrequent bus service you may well have to get back to town by taxi. **Geraki**, at the tip of the peninsula has another long, lovely stretch of sandy beach.

The Southern Peninsula

On the map, Zakynthos looks like a piranha with gaping jaws, about to devour the crumb-sized islets of **Marathonissi** and **Pelouza**, the latter colonized in 1473 BC by King Zakynthos. Today both are rich fishing grounds. **Kalamaki** has a sandy beach under Mt Skopos, at the beginning of currant country. The next town, **Lagana**, is Zakynthos' most developed resort, a favourite both of British and German package tourists and families over for the weekend from the Peloponnese. The fine sandy beach overlooks some curious rock formations by the sea—a beach also popular as an egg-laying ground for loggerhead turtles. It became the centre of an international stir when environmentalists themselves were at loggerheads with government ministries and the island tourist industry to protect the fragile beach areas the turtles have for generations used as hatcheries. Uncompensated for the beaches they owned, some Zantiots even resorted to setting fires on them to keep the turtles away; in 1992 the World Wide Fund for Nature purchased 30 hectares of nesting beach and hired wardens to watch over them.

Behind Lagana extends the **plain of Zakynthos**, a lovely region to cycle through with its old country estates. Further south is **Keri**, with another sandy beach below but it's best known for its nearby **Pissa tou Keriou**: natural pitch wells, used, as in ancient times, to caulk boats. These were well known in antiquity, referred to by both Herodotos and Pliny. There are tavernas by the beach and fine views from the village of Keri.

North, in the central cluster of farming villages, **Macherado** stands out with its lovely church of **Ag. Mavra**, with a beautiful old icon of the saint and church bells noted for their musical quality. In nearby **Lagopoda** there is also the pretty Eleftherias monastery.

Ag. Nikolaos is a very pretty village overlooking the plain from the west; on the main inland road northwest of Zakynthos town is **Katastari**, the island's second largest town, marking the northern edge of the plain. Below Katastari, **Alikes** marks the beginning of a wonderful long stretch of sand which continues west around the bay to **Alikanes**. From Katastari you can take a taxi up to **Anafoni-tria** and its monastery, a rare survivor of the earthquake, with frescoes and the cell of Ag. Dionysos (d. 1622) and a medieval tower.

Unlike the low rolling hills and plain of the east, the west coast of Zakynthos plunges steeply and abruptly into the sea. It does, however, have many caves. **Ag. Gerasimou, Xinthia** (track from Anafonitria) with sulphur springs—evidence of the island's volcanic origins—and **Sklavou** are the most interesting, excluding of course **Kianoun Cave**, the local rival for Capri's Blue Grotto, glowing with every imaginable shade of blue. Kianoun can be visited by caique, either from Zakynthos town or Alikes. The largest village on the west coast is **Volimes**; to go swimming there wear swim shoes, so hot are the rocks and sand. **Ano Volimes** just above it is a pretty little mountain village.

A small islet some 50km south of Zakynthos, called **Strophades**, has a Byzantine monastery which served as a fortress for many years, until the Saracens finally overcame the defence of the monks and plundered it. Today only the building remains, and a lighthouse. The island is a popular resting station for migratory doves. If you have your own boat and have been looking for an out-of-the-way, romantic destination you won't find a better one.

Festivals

A carnival initiated by the Venetians remains strong in Zakynthos and lasts for two weeks prior to Lent, known for its masked singers and dancing. For the *paniyiri* of Ag. Dimitriou on 24 August and 17 December, Zakynthos town is strewn with myrtle and there are fireworks at the church. During Holy Week the inhabitants also give themselves over to an infectious merriment. Slightly more modest is Zoodochos Pigi in the town on 10 November. In July the Zakynthia takes place with cultural activities; at the end of August and beginning of September, the International Meeting of Medieval and Popular Theatre, with daily performances.

(0695–) **Where to Stay**

There are hotels in town and around the island in about equal proportion, although it's more pleasant to stay outside the centre.

expensive

In Zakynthos town, you can choose between the **Strada Marina** at 14 K. Lombardou St, © 22 761, nicely located on the quay. A little more expensive is the **Reparo** at Roma and Voultsou St, © 23 578, clean, pleasant and friendly. **Alfa** on Tertseti St, © 26 641, has bungalows for about the same price. Outside the town, most of the accommodation is at Lagana, which has the giant **Zante Beach**, © 51 130, with pool and tennis. In Tragaki the A class **Caravel** (sister to the one in Athens) will lighten your wallet, but it has all the trimmings, © 25 261, as does the new **Plagos Beach** at Tsilivi, © 24 147.

moderate

Zakynthos town has nothing outstanding in this category. Two decently priced places are **Ionion**, 18 A. Roma, © 23 739, and **Dessy**, 73 N. Koliva, © 28 505. There are almost 20 class C hotels in Lagana, scores of rooms to rent and the people to fill them up. Unless you like that sort of thing, head to more serene haunts such as Planos where the C class **Cosmopolite**, © 28 752, has 14 good rooms, Tsilivi (**Orea Heleni**, © 28 788), Vassiliki (**Porto Roma**, © 22 781), or Keri, which is serene and has the cheapest rooms on the island.

Zakynthos   153

Simple rooms are mostly available in Zakynthos town and Lagana, although you can find simple accommodation elsewhere—Keri, for example, is tranquil, and has some of the cheapest rooms on the island. If you have any difficulty, the tourist police off the Plateia Solomou have a list of rooms to let. There are **campsites** at Tsilivi, Lagana, Gerakari and near Lithakia.

Eating Out

In Zakynthos town, you can eat well at **P. Evangelos** on Alex Roma St for 2500 dr.; the food is freshly prepared and good. There are several expensive places on Ag. Marko square and one that's not, **Boukios**, serving reliable Greek fare for around 2500 dr. Other moderate restaurants can be found near the city hall. The **Panorama** is in a lovely spot up by the castle, and you can listen to live Cantada music while indulging in some traditional Zantiote dishes such as rabbit casserole or *mouskari kokkinisto*, beef in tomato sauce (2500–3000 dr.). On the road to Argassi, near the church of Ag. Dionysos, **Karavomilos** has the name for the best fish on the island (3500 dr.). For more dining with a view, there's **Alla** up on Filikon 38, located in one of the few houses to have survived the earthquake (2000–3000 dr.). Lagana has a host of restaurants, both Greek and international, and many British pubs serving bar food.

BC

7000–2800	Neolithic Era
4000	Precocious civilization at Palaeochoe, Limnos
3000	Milos exports obsidian
3000–2000	Early Cycladic civilization
2800–1000	Bronze Age
2600–2000	Early Minoan civilization in Crete
2000–1700	Middle Minoan: Cretan thalassocracy rules the Aegean
1700–1450	Late Minoan
1600–1150	Mycenaean civilization begins with invasion of the Peloponnese
c.1450	Eruption of Santorini's volcano decimates the Minoans; Mycenaeans occupy ruined Crete and Rhodes
1180	Traditional date of the fall of Troy (4 July)
c.1150	Beginning of the dark ages: Dorian invasion disrupts Mycenaean culture; Ionians settle Asia Minor and islands.
1000	Kos and the three cities of Rhodes join Doric Hexapolis
1100–100	Iron Age
1100–700	Geometric Period
700–500	Archaic Period
650	Aegina is first in Greece to mint coins
Late 600s	Sappho born on Lesbos
570–480	Pythagoras of Samos
500–323	Classical Age
490–479	Persian Wars end with defeat of Persian army and fleet
478	Delos becomes HQ of the Athenian-dominated Maritime League
460–377	Hippocrates of Kos
431–404	Peloponnesian War cripples Athens
378	Second Delian League
338	Philip of Macedon conquers Athens and the rest of Greece
334–323	Conquests of Alexander the Great
323–146	Hellenistic Age
146–AD 410	Roman Age

Chronology

88	Mithridates of Pontus, enemy of Rome, devastates many islands
86	Romans under Sulla destroy Athens and other Greek rebels who supported Mithridates

AD

58	St Paul visits Lindos, Rhodes
95	St John the Divine writes the Apocalypse on Patmos
391	Paganism outlawed in Roman Empire

410–1453	Byzantine Era
727–843	Iconoclasm in the Eastern Church
824–861	Saracen/Arab Occupation
961	Emperor Nikephoros Phokas reconquers Crete from the Saracens
1054	Pope ex-communicates Patriarch of Constantinople over differences in the creed
1088	Foundation of the Monastery on Patmos
1204	Venetians lead Fourth Crusade conquest of Contantinople and take the islands as their share of the booty
1261	Greeks retake Constantinople from Latins
1309	Knights of St John, chased out of Jerusalem, establish on Rhodes
1453	Turks begin conquest of Greece
1522	Ottomans defeat Knights of St John
1541	El Greco born on Crete
1669	Venetians lose Herakleon, Crete to the Turks after a 20-year siege
1771–74	Catherine the Great sends Russian fleet into the Aegean to harry the Sultan
1796	Napoleon captures Venice and her Ionian islands
1815–64	British rule Ionian islands
1821–27	Greek War of Independence begins
1823	Aegina made the capital of free Greece
1827	Annihilation of Turkish fleet by the British, French and Russian allies at the Battle of Navarino
1833	Otho of Bavaria becomes the first king of the Greeks
1883–1957	Cretan writer Nikos Kazantzakis
1912–13	Balkan Wars give Greece Macedonia, Crete and the Northeast Aegean Islands; the Italians pick up the Dodecanese
1922–23	Greece invades Turkey with catastrophic results
1924	Greece becomes a republic
1935	Restoration of the monarchy
1941	Nazi paratroopers complete first ever invasion by air on Crete
1945	Treaty signed returning Dodecanese islands to Greece
1948	Dodecanese islands reunite with Greece
1949	End of civil war between communists and US-backed government
1953	Earthquake shatters the Ionian islands
1967	Colonels' coup establishes a dictatorship
1974	Failure of the Junta's Cyprus adventure leads to the regime's collapse and restoration of democracy
1981	First-ever nominally socialist government (PASOK) elected
1983	Greece joins the EEC
1990	PASOK lose election to conservative New Democracy (ND)
1993	PASOK re-elected

Language

157

Although modern Greek, or Romaíka is a minor language spoken by few non-Greeks, it has the distinction of having caused riots and the fall of a government (in 1901). In Greece today there are basically two languages, the purist or katharevóusa and the popular or demotikí. Both are developments of ancient Greek, but although the purist is consciously Classical, the popular is as close to its ancient origins as French is to Latin. While many purist words are common in the speech of the people, the popular dominates, especially in the countryside.

Until the turn of the century all literature appeared in the purist language. What shook Athens with riots in 1901 was the appearance of the Iliad and the New Testament in the demotic. When the fury had died down a bit, more and more writers were found to be turning their pens to the demotic. Cavafy, the first great modern Greek poet, wrote in both the popular and purist. In its 'moral cleansing' of Greece the Papadopoulos government tried to revive the purist, but with little success.

Knowing the language of any country makes the stay twice as enjoyable; in Greece, especially, people spend much of the day talking. But modern Greek isn't a particularly easy language to pick by ear, and it is often spoken at great velocity (if you speak slowly someone is sure to interrupt). If you buy a modern Greek grammar, check to see if it has the demotic and not just the purist. Even if you have no desire to learn Greek, it is helpful to know at least the alphabet—so that you can find your way around—and a few basic words and phrases.

The Greek Alphabet

			Pronunciation/English Equivalent
A	α	*álfa*	short 'a' as in 'father'
B	β	*víta*	v
Γ	γ	*gámma*	gutteral *g* or *y* sound
Δ	δ	*thélta*	hard *th* as in 'though'
E	ε	*épsilon*	short 'e' as in 'bet'
Z	ζ	*zíta*	z
H	η	*íta*	long 'e' as in 'bee'
Θ	θ	*thíta*	soft *th* as in 'thin'

I	ι	*yóta*	long 'e' as in 'bee';
			sometimes like the 'y' in 'yet'
K	κ	*káppa*	k
Λ	λ	*lámtha*	l
M	μ	*mi*	m
N	ν	*ni*	n
Ξ	ξ	*ksi*	'x' as in 'ox'
O	ο	*ómicron*	'o' as in 'cot'
Π	π	*pi*	p
P	ρ	*ro*	r
Σ	σ	*sígma*	s
T	τ	*taf*	t
Υ	υ	*ípsilon*	long 'e' as in 'bee'
Φ	φ	*fi*	f
X	χ	*chi*	German *ch* as in 'doch'
Ψ	ψ	*psi*	*ps* as in 'stops'
Ω	ω	*oméga*	'o' as in 'cot'

Dipthongs and Consonant Combinations

AI	αι	short 'e' as in 'bet'
EI	ει, OI οι	'i' as in 'machine'
OΥ	ου	*oo* as in 'too'
AΥ	αυ	*av* or *af*
EΥ	ευ	*ev* or *ef*
HΥ	ηυ	*iv* or *if*
ΓΓ	γγ	*ng* as in 'angry'
ΓK	γκ	hard 'g'; *ng* within word
NT	ντ	'd'; *nd* within word
MΠ	μπ	'b'; *mp* within word

Vocabulary

Yes	*né*	Ναί
	(with a short nod or tilt of the head)	
	málista (formal)	Μάλιστα
No	óchi	Οχι
	(with a backwards jerk of the head, with a click of the tongue, smack of the lips or raise of the eyebrows)	

I don't know	then xéro	Δέν ξέρω
	(An even greater throwing back of the head, or a display of empty hands)	
I don't understand ... (Greek)	then katalavéno ... (elliniká)	Δέν καταλαβαίνω ... (Ελληνικά)
Does someone speak English?	milái kanis angliká?	Μιλάει κανείς αγγλικά;
Go away	fíyete	Φύγετε
Help!	voíthia!	Βοήθεια!
My friend	o fílos moo (m)	Ο φίλος μου
	ee fíli moo (f)	Η φίλη μου
Please	parakaló	Παρακαλώ
Thank you	evcharistó	Ευχαριστώ
(very much)	(pára polí)	(πάρα πολύ)
You're welcome	parakaló	Παρακαλώ
It doesn't matter	then pirázi	Δέν πιράζει
Alright	en daxi	Εν τάξι
Of course	vevéos	Βεβαίος
Excuse me	signómi	Συγνώμη
Pardon?	oríste?	Ορίστε;
Be careful!	proséchete!	Προσέχεται!
Nothing	típota	Τίποτα
What is your name?	pos sas léne? (formal)	Πώς σάς λένε;
	pos se léne?	Πώς σέ λένε;
How are you?	ti kánete? (formal/pl)	Τί κάνεται;
	ti kanis?	Τί κάνεις;
Hello	yásas, hérete (formal/pl)	Γειάσας, Χέρεται
	yásou	Γειάσου
Goodbye	yásas, hérete (formal/pl)	Γειάσας, Χέρεται
	yásou, adío	Γειάσου, Αντίο
Good morning	kaliméra	Καλημέρα
Good evening	kalispéra	Καλησπέρα
Good night	kaliníchta	Καληνύχτα
What is that?	ti íne aftó?	Τί είναι αυτό;
What?	ti?	Τί;
Who?	piós? (m), piá? (f)	Ποιός; Ποιά;

Where?	poo?	Ποιός;
When?	póte?	Πότε;
why?	yiatí?	Γιατί;
how?	pos?	Πώς;
I am	íme	Είμαι
You are (sing)	ísse	Είσε
He, she, it is	íne	Είναι
We are	ímaste	Είμαστε
You are (pl)	íssaste	Είσαστε
They are	íne	Είναι
I have	écho	Εχω
You have (sing)	échis	Εχεις
He, she, it has	échi	Εχει
We have	échome	Εχομαι
You have (pl)	échete	Εχεται
They have	échoon	Εχουν
I am lost	échasa to thrómo	Εχασα το δρόμο
I am hungry	pinó	Πεινώ
I am thirsty	thipsó	Διψώ
I am tired	íme kourasménos	Είμαι κουρασμένος
I am sleepy	nistázo	Νυστάζω
I am ill	íme árostos	Είμαι άρρωστος
I am poor	íme ftochós	Είμαι φτωχός
I love you	s'agapó	Σ'αγαπώ
good	kaló	καλό
bad	kakó	κακό
so-so	étsi kétsi	έτσι κ'έτσι
slowly	sigá sigá	σιγά σιγά
fast	grígora	γρήγορα
big	megálo	μεγάλο
small	mikró	μικρό
hot	zestó	ζεστό
cold	crío	κρίο

Shops, Services, Sightseeing

I would like …	*tha íthela …*	Θά ήθελα …
where is …?	*poo íne …?*	Πού είναι …;
how much is it?	*póso káni?*	Πόσο κάνει;
bakery	*fournos*	φούρνος
	artopiíon (antiquated, above entrance)	Αρτοποιείον
bank	*trápeza*	τράπεζα
beach	*paralía*	παραλία
bed	*kreváti*	κρεβάτι
book	*vivlío*	βιβλίο
bookshop	*vivliopolío*	βιβλιοπολείο
butcher	*kreopolío*	κρεοπωλείο
church	*eklisía*	εκκλησία
cinema	*kinimatográfos*	κινηματογράφος
food	*fayitó*	φαγητό
hospital	*nosokomío*	νοσοκομείο
hotel	*xenodochío*	ξενοδοχείο
hot water	*zestó neró*	ζεστό νερό
house	*spíti*	σπίτι
kiosk	*períptero*	περίπτερο
money	*leftá*	λεφτά
museum	*moosío*	μουσείο
music	*musikí*	μουσική
newspaper (foreign)	*efimerítha (xéni)*	εφημερίδα (ξένη)
pharmacy	*farmakío*	φαρμακείο
police station	*astinomía*	αστυνομία
policeman	*astifílakas*	αστιφύλακας
post office	*tachithromío*	ταχυδρομείο
restaurant	*estiatório*	εστιατόριο
ruins	*archéa*	αρχαία
sea	*thálassa*	θάλασσα
shoe store	*papootsís*	παπουτσής
shower	*doush*	ντούς
student	*fititís*	φοιτητής
telephone office	*OTE*	OTE
theatre	*théatro*	θέατρο

toilet	*tooaléta*	τουαλέττα
tourist policeman	*astifílakas tooristikís*	αστιφύλακας τουριστικής
a walk	*vólta*	βόλτα

Time

What time is it?	*ti óra íne?*	Τί ώρα είναι;
month	*mína*	μήνα
week	*evthomáda*	εβδομάδα
day	*méra*	μέρα
morning	*proí*	πρωί
afternoon	*apóyevma*	απόγευμα
evening	*vráthi*	βράδυ
yesterday	*chthés*	χθές
today	*símera*	σήμερα
tomorrow	*ávrio*	αύριο
now	*tóra*	τώρα
later	*metá*	μετά
it is early	*íne norís*	είναι νωρίς
it is late	*íne argá*	είναι αργά

Travel Directions

I want to go to ...	*thélo na páo sto (m), sti (f) ...*	Θέλω νά πάω στό, στη ...;
How can I get to ...?	*pós boró na páo sto (m), sti (f) ...?*	Πώς μπορώ νά πάω στό, στη ...;
Can you give me a ride to ...?	*boréte na me páte sto (m), sti (f) ...?*	Μπορείτε νά μέ πάτε στό, στή ...;
Where is ...?	*poo íne ...?*	Πού είναι ...;
How far is it?	*póso makriá íne?*	Πόσο μακριά είναι;
When will the ... come?	*póte tha érthi to (n), ee (f), o (m) ...?*	Πότε θά έρθη τό, ή, ό ...;
When will the ... leave?	*póte tha fíyí to (n), ee (f), o (m) ...?*	Πότε θά φύγη τό, ή, ό ...;
From where do I catch ...?	*apó poo pérno ...?*	Από πού πέρνω ...;
How long does the trip take?	*póso keró pérni to taxíthi?*	Πόσο καιρό πέρνει τό ταξίδι;

Please show me	*parakaló thíkstemoo*	Παρακαλώ δείξτε μου
How much is it?	*póso káni?*	Πόσο κάνει;
the (nearest) town	*to horió (to pió kondinó)*	Το χωριό (το πιό κοντινό)
Have a good trip	*kaló taxíthi*	Καλό ταξίδι
here	*ethó*	εδώ
there	*ekí*	εκεί
near	*kondá*	κοντά
far	*makriá*	μακριά
full	*yemáto*	γεμάτο
left	*aristerá*	αριστερά
right	*thexiá*	δεξιά
forward	*brostá*	μροστά
back	*píso*	πίσω
north	*vória*	βόρεια
south	*nótia*	νότια
east	*anatoliká*	ανατολικά
west	*thitiká*	δυτικά
corner	*goniá*	γωνιά
square	*platía*	πλατεία

Driving

where can I rent ...?	*poo boró na nikiáso ...?*	Πού μποπώ νά νοικιάσω ...;
a car	*éna aftokínito*	ένα αυτοκινητο
a motorbike	*éna michanáki*	ένα μηχανάκι
a bicycle	*éna pothílato*	ένα ποδήλατο
where can I buy petrol?	*poo boró nagorásso venzíni?*	Πού μπορώ ν΄αγοράσω βενζίνη;
where is a garage?	*poo íne éna garáz?*	Πού είναι ένα γκαράζ;
a mechanic	*énan mikanikó*	έναν μηχανικό
a map	*enan chárti*	έναν χάρτη
where is the road to ...?	*poo íne o thrómos yiá ...?*	Πού είναι ο δρόμος γιά ...;
where does this road lead?	*poo pái aftós o thrómos?*	Πού πάει αυτός ο δρόμος;
is the road good?	*íne kalós o thrómos?*	Είναι καλός ο δρόμος;

EXIT	*éxothos*	ΕΞΟΔΟΣ
ENTRANCE	*ísothos*	ΕΙΣΟΔΟΣ
DANGER	*kínthinos*	ΚΙΝΔΥΝΟΣ
SLOW	*argá*	ΑΡΓΑ
NO PARKING	*apagorévete ee státhmevsis*	ΑΠΑΓΟΡΕΥΕΤΑΙ Η ΣΤΑΘΜΕΥΣΙΣ
KEEP OUT	*apagorévete ee ísothos*	ΑΠΑΓΟΡΕΥΕΤΑΙ Η ΕΙΣΟΔΟΣ

Numbers

one	*énas* (*m*), *mía* (*f*), *éna* (*n*)	ένας, μία, ένα
two	*thío*	δύο
three	*tris* (*m, f*), *tría* (*n*)	τρείς, τρία
four	*téseris* (*m, f*), *téssera* (*n*)	τέσσερεις, τέσσερα
five	*pénde*	πέντε
six	*éxi*	έξι
seven	*eptá*	επτά
eight	*októ*	οκτώ
nine	*ennéa*	εννέα
ten	*théka*	δέκα
eleven	*éntheka*	έντεκα
twelve	*thótheka*	δώδεκα
thirteen	*thekatría*	δεκατρία
fourteen	*thekatéssera*	δεκατέσσερα
twenty	*íkosi*	είκοσι
twenty-one	*íkosi éna* (*m, n*) *mía* (*f*)	είκοσι ένα, μία
thirty	*triánda*	τριάντα
forty	*saránda*	σαράντα
fifty	*penínda*	πενήντα
sixty	*exínda*	εξήντα
seventy	*evthomínda*	ευδομήντα
eighty	*ogthónda*	ογδόντα
ninety	*enenínda*	ενενήντα
one hundred	*ekató*	εκατό
one thousand	*chília*	χίλια

Months/Days

January	*Ianooários*	Ιανουάριος
February	*Fevrooários*	Φεβουάριος
March	*Mártios*	Μάρτιος
April	*Aprílios*	Απρίλιος
May	*Máios*	Μάιος
June	*Ioónios*	Ιούνιος
July	*Ioólios*	Ιούλιος
August	*Avgoostos*	Αύγουστος
September	*Septémvrios*	Σεπτέμβριος
October	*Októvrios*	Οκτώβριος
November	*Noémvrios*	Νοέμβριος
December	*Thekémvrios*	Δεκέμβριος

Sunday	*Kiriakí*	Κυριακή
Monday	*Theftéra*	Δευτέρα
Tuesday	*Tríti*	Τρίτη
Wednesday	*Tetárti*	Τετάρτη
Thursday	*Pémpti*	Πέμπτη
Friday	*Paraskeví*	Παρασκευή
Saturday	*Sávato*	Σάββατο

Transport

the airport	*to arothrómio*	τό αεροδρόμιο
the aeroplane	*to aropláno*	τό αεροπλάνο
the bus station	*ee stási leoforíou*	ή στάση λεωφορείου
the bus	*to leoforío*	τό λεωφορείο
the railway station	*o stathmós too trénou*	ό σταθμός τού τραίνου
the train	*to tréno*	τό τραίνο
the port	*to limáni*	τό λιμάνι
the port authority	*to limenarchío*	τό λιμεναρχείο
the ship	*to plío, to karávi*	τό πλοίο, τό καράβι
the steamship	*to vapóri*	τό βαπόρι
the car	*to aftokínito*	τό αυτοκίνητο
a ticket	*éna isitírio*	ένα εισιτήριο

The Menu

Hors d'oeuvres	Orektiká (Mezéthes)	Ορεκτικά (Μεζέδεs)
yoghurt and cucumbers	tzatziki	τζατζίκι
olives	eliés	ελης̓ές
stuffed vine leaves	dolmáthes	ντολμάδεs
cod's roe dip	taramosalata	ταραμοσαλάτα
mixed hors d'oeuvres	thiáfora orektiká	διάφορα ορεκτικά

Soups	Soópes	Σούπεs
egg and lemon soup	avgolémono	αυγολέμονο
vegetable soup	chortósoupa	χορτόσουπα
fish soup	psarósoupa	ψαρόσουπα
giblets in egg and lemon soup	magirítsa	μαγειρίτσα

Pasta and Rice	Zimariká	Ζυμαρικά
pilaf	piláfi	πιλάφι
spaghetti	spagéti	σπαγκέτι
macaroni	makarónia	μακαρόνια

Vegetables (in oil)	Latherá	Λαδερά
potatoes	patátes	πατάτεs
stuffed tomatoes	tomátes yemistés	ντομάτεs γεμιστέs
stuffed aubergines/ eggplants	melitzánes yemistés	μελιτζάνεs γεμιστέs
stuffed peppers	piperíes yemistés	πιπεριέs γεμιστέs
beans	fasólia	φασόλια
lentils	fakí	φακή
greens	chórta	χόρτα

Fish	Psária	Ψάρια
lobster	astakós	αστακός
little squid	kalamarákia	καλαμαράκια
octopus	achtapóthi	αχταπόδι
red mullet	barboúni	μπαρμπούνι
prawns (shrimps)	garíthes	γαρίδεs
whitebait	maríthes	μαρίδεs
sea bream	sinagrítha	συναγρίδα

fried cod (with garlic and vinegar sauce)	bakaliáros (skorthaliá)	μπακαλιάρος (σκορδαλιά)
oysters	stríthia	στρείδια
bass	lithrínia	λιθρίνια

Eggs — Avgá — Αυγά

ham omelette	omeléta me zambón	ομελέττα μέ ζαμπόν
cheese omelette	omeléta me tirí	ομελέττα μέ τυρί
fried (scrambled) eggs	avgá tiganitá (brouyé)	αυγά τηγανιτά (μπρουγέ)

Main Courses — Kíria Piáta — Κύρια Πιάτα

chicken	kotópoulo	κοτόπουλο
beefsteak	biftéki	μπιφτέκι
rabbit	kounéli	κουνέλι
meat and macaroni	pastítsio	παστίτσιο
meat and aubergine/ eggplant with white sauce	mousaká	μουσακά
liver	seekóti	συκώτι
veal	moschári	μοσχάρι
lamb	arnáki	αρνάκι
pork chops	brizólas chirinés	μπριζόλες χοιρινές
meat balls in tomato sauce	soutsoukákia	σουτζουκάκια
sausage	lukániko	λουκάνικο

Grills — Skáras — Σχάρας

meat on a skewer	souvláki	σουβλάκι
veal chops	kotelétes	κοτελέτες
roast chicken	kotópoulo psistó	κοτόπουλο ψηστό
meat balls	keftéthes	κεφτέδες

Salads — Salátes — Σαλάτες

tomatoes	domátes	ντομάτες
cucumber	angoúri	αγγούρι
Russian salad	róssiki saláta	ρώσσικη σαλάτα

| village salad with cheese and olives | *choriatiki* | χοριάτικη |
| courgettes/zucchini | *kolokithákia* | κολοκυθάκια |

Cheeses	**Tiriá**	**Τυριά**
cheese pie	*tirópitta*	τυρόπιττα
goat's cheese	*féta*	φέτα
hard buttery cheese	*kasséri*	κασέρι
blue cheese (roquefort)	*rokfór*	ροκφόρ
Greek 'Gruyère'	*graviéra*	γραβιέρα

Sweets	**Glyká**	**Γλυκά**
ice cream	*pagotó*	παγωτό
sugared biscuits	*kourabiéthes*	κουραμπιέδες
hot honey fritters	*loukoumáthes*	λουκουμάδες
sesame seed sweet	*halvá*	χαλβά
nuts and honey in fillo pastry	*baklavá*	μπακλαβά
custard in fillo pastry	*galaktoboúreko*	γαλακτομπούρεκο
yoghurt	*yiaoúrti*	γιαούρτι
rice pudding	*rizógalo*	ρυζόγαλο
shredded wheat with nuts and honey	*kataifi*	καταΐφι
custard tart	*bougátsa*	μπουγάτσα
soft almond biscuits	*amigthalotá*	αμιγδαλωτά

Fruit	**Froóta**	**Φρούτα**
pear	*achláthi*	αχλάδι
orange	*portokáli*	πορτοκάλι
apple	*mílo*	μήλο
peach	*rothákino*	ροδάκινο
melon	*pepóni*	πεπόνι
watermelon	*karpoúzi*	καρπούζι
plum	*thamáskino*	δαμάσκινο
figs	*síka*	σύκα
grapes	*stafília*	σταφύλια
banana	*banána*	μπανάνα
apricot	*veríkoko*	βερύκοκο

Miscellaneous

water (boiled)	*neró (vrastó)*	νερό (βραστό)
bread	*psomí*	ψωμί
butter	*voútiro*	βούτυρο
honey	*méli*	μέλι
jam	*marmelátha*	μαρμελάδα
salt	*aláti*	αλάτι
pepper	*pipéri*	πιπερι
sugar	*záchari*	ζάχαρη
oil	*láthi*	λάδι
vinegar	*xíthi*	ξύδι
mustard	*mustárda*	μουστάρδα
lemon	*lemóni*	λεμόνι
milk	*gála*	γάλα
tea	*tsái*	τσάϊ
chocolate	*sokoláta*	σοκολάτα
the bill/check	*logariasmó*	λογαριασμό
to your health!	*stín iyásas (formal, pl)*	στήν ηγειά σας!
	stín iyásou (sing)	στήν ηγειά σου!

Note: Page references in **bold** indicate main references and those in *italics* indicate
maps. Ionian Islands appear in capital letters.

Index